FASTER, SMARTER, HIGHER

Utkarsh Rai is Vice President Software, Infinera and Managing Director, Infinera India. He is also an angel investor for startups. Utkarsh is a recipient of the Udyog Rattan Award and has several books under his belt. He is passionate about many things in his life like globetrotting, learning about different histories and cultures, and fitness. For more information, contact him at utkarshrai@yahoo.com or visit http://www.utkarshrai.com.

FASTER, SMARTER, HIGHER

MANAGING YOUR CAREER

PLUS 51 INSIGHTS FROM
BUSINESS LEADERS

UTKARSH RAI

RUPA

Published by
Rupa Publications India Pvt. Ltd. 2016
7/16, Ansari Road, Daryaganj
New Delhi 110002

Sales centres:

Allahabad Bengaluru Chennai
Hyderabad Jaipur Kathmandu
Kolkata Mumbai

ISBN: 978-81-291-3750-0

Second impression 2016

10 9 8 7 6 5 4 3 2

To
Professionals of the Twenty-first Century

CONTENTS

Introduction   *xi*

1. Managing Self
  1. Goals Versus Dreams   1
  2. Twists And Turns   5
  3. Self Goal > Organization Goal?   10
  4. The Ethical Conundrum   13
  5. Are You Ready To Step Up?   16
  6. A Mentor Is Better Than a Godfather   19
  7. You, the Brand   22
  8. Visibility Matters   25
  9. Be Networked   28
  10. Mr High Maintenance   31
  11. Grooming Quotient   34

2. Managing Your Manager
  12. The Man Friday   38
  13. Winning Your Manager   43
  14. Understanding Your Manager   46

15. Tuning Into Your Manager's Frequency   52
16. Manager-cum-owner   60
17. Manager's Friends, Enemies And Frenemies   63
18. Saying No To Your Manager   64
19. Hating Your Manager   68

3. Managing Your Team
20. Apple Among Oranges   73
21. Perform Or...   77
22. What Employees Want   82
23. Gauging the Pulse   86
24. Employee Is the King   89
25. Playing Fair   92

4. Managing Your Peers
26. Peer Pressure   96
27. Difficult Peer   99
28. Peer Power   100
29. Watching Your Back   104
30. Peer Fear   107
31. Peeritism   110

5. Managing Your Manager's Boss
32. The Big Boss   113
33. The Future Boss   115
34. Boss Almighty   118
35. Appraising the Appraisal   121
36. Help!   125
37. A View From the Top   128
38. Manager And You   132

6. Managing Manager's Peers **138**

   39. Seeking Sponsors 138

   40. Building Bridges 141

   41. Safeguarding Your Interests 143

   42. Reaching Out 146

   43. Identifying Your Fallback 148

   44. Roadblock 150

7. Managing Others **153**

   45. Be On the Right Side Of the HR 153

   46. Big Brother Is Watching You 156

   47. A Penny Saved Is a Penny Earned 159

   48. Customer Is the Emperor 161

   49. Knowing Your Vendors 165

8. Managing the Acrobatics of Future

   50. You Are a Product 171

   51. Extending Your Shelf Life 174

Acknowledgements 178

INTRODUCTION

Many bright people do not reach the position they deserve simply because they lack the realization that by confining themselves in their cubicles and focusing narrowly on their work they could earn kudos only in the beginning of their career but not later. Some of them are puzzled at how even being on the right side of their managers is still not helping them to grow. Some are frustrated because even though they work very hard, they are neither compensated well nor given better opportunities. Some are not able to cope up with their difficult colleagues while others don't know how and when to say no to their managers. Then there are those who become very nervous in front of their manager's bosses as they are unsure about how to say things without hurting their managers. These woes are plenty and are not necessarily just about junior employees, but managers too. Managers have unfair expectations like demanding respect from their teams but not doing enough to earn it. Many of them focus only on managing upwards failing to realize that managing downwards is equally important.

Hard work is necessary for a job, but not sufficient to grow in your career. You must realize that over the years, several other skills start to play a role in addition to your subject matter expertise. Being in a hurry to rise, don't ignore the need of honing your other skills, as sooner or later you will start cribbing about being treated unfairly. It is during such phases that you start committing blunders further putting a brake in your career growth.

Workplace dynamics are constantly changing. Unlike the new employees, those who have stayed longer fail to come to terms about these changing dynamics. Don't be one of them. Don't try to solve new challenges with your same old behaviour because you will fail and then point fingers at the company for being side-lined. This lack of such understanding leads to angst about losing out in the corporate race. Frustration sets in but there is hardly any realization of what could be done differently.

This book addresses career management from the perspective of managing key relationships at work and is divided into chapters on how to deal with various stakeholders of your career. Relationships that can help you learn, realize and correct mistakes, and understand others' perspectives on problem solving. You can also leverage the key people's position in the company to seek out advice and mentor you in enriching your career. They can pinpoint your blind spots and help you to decide courses, trainings and feedback to make you more effective. Successful management of key relationships will also help you to adapt to the dynamic ecosystem and play a vital role in deciding or supporting your career growth.

Any relationship management has to start first with the self and that is what is discussed in Chapter 1. You spend most of your time on thinking about others, but hardly any time on self-realization and taking steps based on that. This chapter covers topics that are important for bettering your self like having a clear goal and building a good brand. People spend innumerable months and sometimes years thinking about what went wrong and how someone else was responsible for their pathetic situation at work, but the truth is that it could just have been a lack of self-awareness on their part.

Chapter 2 talks about the most favourite of all workplace discussions—yes, it is about managers! You have all spent enough hours talking about how they should see things the way you see them, and how they should respond the way you want them to respond. This section gives you practical tips on how you can manage your manager.

Chapter 3 deals with how to manage your team effectively. As employees look towards their manager for growth in their career, those who are in a management role need to look both at the manager and his team members. Managing people is an art and even the most successful of managers sometimes gets stuck because they have not been able to manage their team effectively.

Chapter 4 talks about a competitive and challenging relationship, that is, how to deal with your peers. All your skills are tested in managing this relationship. Peers are neither your managers nor do they work for you. Even if they are not directly related to your career, they can enhance or spoil your career. It is a tender relationship that must be nurtured.

Chapter 5 talks about managing your manager's boss. You may tend to be scared to approach him because you are worried about how it will be perceived. Besides, you may be apprehensive about what his manager will think of such a meeting. You like many understand the importance of such relationships, but self-doubt and myths might hinder your approach. This chapter talks about the role your manager's boss plays in your work life and how you can leverage it to your advantage.

Chapter 6 talks about managing your manager's peer. This relationship is highly underutilized because people fail to see its potential. Of course, it requires a highly skilled approach and this chapter describes how to hone this art and lists the benefits in doing so.

Chapter 7 talks about how the support functions HR, Finance, IT, Admin., etc., impact your career negatively, if not managed well. This chapter talks about dos and don'ts in managing such interactions.

The last chapter talks about acrobatics of future. It discusses how to manage your career in times when on one hand longevity has increased and on the other hand your ability to remain employable for longer period of time has reduced.

Although the book is written in masculine gender for the purpose of uniformity, it is applicable to all. It will enable your career to grow 'faster' by adopting the 'smarter' approaches mentioned in it and thereby help you in realizing your 'higher' dreams. The book is based on my interactions with over thousands of professionals. Observing them keenly on how they struggle to realize their career goals has helped me to write this book.

CHAPTER ONE

MANAGING SELF

1. GOALS VERSUS DREAMS

What is your career goal? It's a million dollar question.

People are quick to respond on what type of car they want or the gadget they prefer, but when it comes to career, many falter. An instant answer could be more money and to occupy your boss's chair.

If you are not clear about what you want, no one can help you however good your manager may be. While it's a fact that it is not possible for everyone to set a long-term goal, but many don't set a goal for themselves for even a few years. Setting up a goal is very important. It could be anything: You may want to be recognized as an expert in a given area. You may want to change your team. You want to change your current company. You want to switch your profession. You want to take a break and enrol yourself for a professional course.

However, to achieve your goals, you tend to forget about

the soft skills required to achieve them. Therefore, you need to set some goals on soft skills for yourself too. Skills such as improving presentation skills, negotiating skills or interpersonal skills, etc., also qualify as goals.

Write your goal based on what *you* want. Don't restrict yourself due to organizational constraint. Never compromise in setting your goal.

If your goal is to see your importance growing in the organization, you need to reach out to your manager to figure out a way to achieve it. Even if your goal is beyond your manager's scope, it is still important to confide in him and seek his help. He could help you to reach out to others in the organization who could guide you.

Sometimes, your organization may not be able to satisfy what your desire. Therefore, it is important that you know the answer now to save time. Talking with others can get you more clarity to help you to modify, change or fine-tune your goal.

After setting your goal, it is important to know how to make it achievable. That can only happen when you have identified the path to it. Make your plan measurable and actionable. You may lose your way halfway if you don't have a clear path. Don't lose confidence and become disheartened at the sight of a few initial hurdles. Be passionate about your goal. Try not to blame others for not being able to realize your own goals. Don't be averse to taking risk and just accepting the status quo. And don't try to ape someone else's career goal and falter, as it was never your own to start with. All plans need to be actionable, and don't be confused about the right time to work towards your goal aka dream. For example, a person who wants to start his own company but is not hungry enough to fulfil his dream will procrastinate. He may have good ideas and skills, but he does not have the courage to pursue it—probably due to the fear of losing the continuous flow of the monthly salary. This is one of the reasons that there is always a higher probability of failure than success in achieving a goal.

Once you have determined a career goal and an actionable career path, it is important to start implementing it. It will not help if you, like most people, keep your career plan a secret or share it with a very limited group of people for fear of it being sabotaged or being mocked at. Discussing your short-term plan with your boss and with some others will help in setting the right expectation. They may be able to give you inputs and point out the direction for you. It is difficult for your manager to gauge your interest if you have not shared your career plan.

The other advantage of publishing your plan is that it provides a common understanding with your stakeholders. For example, if your plan includes trying a latest technology or starting a new company or taking up a course, you may attract others who have a similar plan and could benefit from their experience or thinking processes. The other advantage in making your plan public is to get early feedback on the feasibility and the timeline of your plan. This can assist you to fine-tune or change your plan right there and then—avoiding the wastage of effort, money and time. The biggest benefit about publishing a plan is that it puts the onus on you to realize it especially because everyone knows about it.

What Can You Do?

It is important that you reflect on what you really want to do.

Identify a few areas for which you have a passion. They will all not become career goals, but it is a good idea to try to develop these passionate ideas. Over time you will be able to start weeding out those for which your passion was superficial. There will be only that one or may be a handful of ideas you want to pursue. Once you shortlist these, do a trial balloon, i.e., run it by your mentor, friend, boss or anyone you think can give you sound advice. You could also approach someone who has expertise in the area for a better insight.

After shortlisting an idea and validating it, the next step is to prepare a career plan, the next milestone in setting your goal. Your plan should have a rough timeline with intermediate milestones. This will help you to stay focused. A fine-tuned career plan is the basis of deciding on whether you can commit to it.

Be prepared to take risks once you start executing your plan. You must evaluate all risks patiently and take corrective actions, if required. Risk assessment is an ongoing process. Risks cannot be identified or resolved at the planning stage itself. Even a foolproof plan is prone to obstacles. But never let obstacles be a deterrent—use them as steps to moving closer to realizing your goal.

Sometimes it happens that you realize that the goal you had set for yourself is not really the right one and that a newer one is more suitable. If you are determined about your new goal, take the plunge and go for it. Don't mope about—just consider it a part of the learning process and move on.

A challenge you may face could be divergent viewpoints on your career goal from friends and family. While some may appreciate your choice, there could be others who could criticize your goal openly. Listen to everyone but ultimately do what your mind and heart tell you to do. If you are not in the profession of your choice, it is high time that you move on to pursue what you really want to do. Money is a big criterion for choosing a career goal, but remember that it is not the sole one. Always remember that many people take salary cuts or leave cushy jobs to pursue their dreams.

People justify their inaction on their goals by citing paucity of time, family responsibilities or lack of financial freedom and many more such reasons. Such reasons could be true for a certain period in your career, but you cannot hide behind these excuses forever. Remember that you can make a new goal for yourself at any stage of your career.

Not only is it important to set a career goal, it is also imperative that you make a plan to achieve it. Review your goal every few years. Make corrections to it, if required, and then proceed. The drive towards achieving your goal, learning during that process and partial achievements, if not all, will certainly trigger happiness and confidence in you to do more and more.

> *Locate your True North even as you begin, lest you regret many years down that you took the wrong train!*
>
> ~PRABIR JHA, GLOBAL CHIEF PEOPLE OFFICER, CIPLA

2. TWISTS AND TURNS

You may think that career growth means to go up the hierarchy of an organization by occupying your manager's chair, and then his boss's chair, and so on. As organizations become leaner, less hierarchical and more flat, going up the ladder has become even slower.

Think about it, when you take a road journey, you don't move at a constant speed—you stop at traffic signals, take diversions, sometimes reach wrong destinations by missing turns, get lost as you misread the map and struggle. Similarly, a career is also full of twists and turns. You need to sense when your path is blocked. Sometimes you become impatient about your career growth and take some steps which in hindsight proved to be less rewarding. If your career plan dictates to take certain steps then you must take it. If you are patient and focus on widening and deepening your skills you may get opportunities to grow in the current team itself. Sometimes attrition of your colleagues, a new exciting project, certain change in company direction, new opportunities, etc., can help in breaking the stagnation too. In spite of all that there could be a situation where you feel stagnant for long. Hence, in order to move up the ladder, you might need to make a lateral shift within your own team, or move to a new team in the same level. Choose the new team where the opportunity to move up is higher. So, rather than waiting and watching, try lateral movement—within or outside the company. Don't be fixated in what you want to do and turn down offers blindly. Evaluate your opportunities with an open mind.

Sometimes when there is reorganization in a company, you may find yourself in a less influential role. You could either choose to live in the past glory of the good old times and curse your fate, or turn this role into a successful one in which you grow exponentially. Always have a will to prove yourself, however bad the times are. If you have been relinquished into a smaller role due to something that you did incorrectly, you need to introspect, perform and then re-launch yourself.

You may feel like giving up your cushy job and taking the plunge into entrepreneurship. The experience in running your own venture and the satisfaction of having followed your passion might be great, but there is a good chance that you might turn out to be unsuccessful. You might need to sell at a loss or simply close down the venture. When you take up a job again, you may not get a better or even the same position you left at. Here again, you need to re-establish yourself before looking for growth. Each and every such experience, step, movement add to the journey of your career.

I am sure that you know by now that growth is non-linear, and those who don't realize it and are not prepared for it will face it with frustration and angst.

What Can You Do?

You need to be hungry for knowledge, passionate about your work and eager to help others. You need to be ready for a rollercoaster ride in your career.

There are many things which are not in your control. It is important to embrace change, however good or bad you feel it is. For example, during restructuring or downsizing, have you heard of any manager voluntarily offering to split his team or relinquish his position to take up a lower one? Most times, it is forced. Certainly you should try to get the best out of any situation, but events do not turn out the way you want and you need to surrender to the new reality. You should, even in the worst of the times, be open to reaching out to people, honest about what has happened and focused on sensing opportunities, rather than thinking about what people will say to the so-called demotion or job loss. Stay positive. It is your career, and only you can take yourself out of it.

It is a human desire to grow in an organization. However, any growth will be short-lived if you do not have the required skills to match the increased responsibilities. So focus on building a high-performing team rather than building a large team. If a large team is not managed well, it reflects poorly on you and will at some point, lead to your unceremonious removal from the position. Also, such restructuring and downsizing will have direct impact on your sphere of control, and therefore you will feel as though you are regressing in your career. It is important that you grow more with the quality of work and the people you hired and groomed, rather than making it a mere quantity game.

Managing a large number of people is a skill in itself. It requires a lot of multiplexing, separating important issues from the irritants, delegating, doing high level risk assessment, and the most important thing is to be on top of major issues and action items. Developing these skills is helpful when you finally start managing a large team.

If you are the type of person who judges growth with money and are constantly looking for jobs that can pay more, then you are prone to making mistakes. By taking up a job just because of higher compensation, with little regard about the nature of work and the opportunity to learn, you may get left behind. Over a period it will become difficult for you to demand a higher compensation due to lack of skills. Over a few years you will feel that the salary hike is not lucrative and the job is not challenging enough, leaving you with a feeling of having wasted your time. Always ensure that you find a job that you like and be prepared to take a salary cut if required. The problem is that a majority of people don't take this step and soon start stagnating.

All organizations and industries go through difficult patches—and this can make your position vulnerable. It is important therefore to remember that you will only be employable when you are flexible about your choice of role and position. Choose a role in which you can learn continuously and a position in which you can contribute significantly.

Be flexible. Don't be fixated on the type of work you want to do. Don't ignore a new opportunity if it is not aligned to your ideas as it could be important for the company. Your stubbornness to be inflexible comes in the way and you can lose tremendous growth opportunity. This lack of flexibility narrows your chance of growth to a huge extent. So the trick is to be flexible in your workplace. Push your obstinacy to one side and volunteer and sign up for additional activities if it is important for the organization. These voluntary activities never go unnoticed.

Take the plunge if you are approached to fill in an internal vacancy. Take some time to think about it. Never give an immediate response because an immediate response might always be 'No', and you could miss an opportunity to grow. It is better to reflect, discuss and weigh your options before deciding. If after all these deliberations, you feel that it is still totally out of your career plan, then it is not wrong to politely refuse. But if it is somewhat overlaps, take the plunge. If you want, you can negotiate for additional benefits at this stage.

Just the way you get frustrated with the speed of the car

in front of you and change your lane to move faster, you need to seek other avenues when you feel blocked in your career. Changing your lane helps you speed up to move to the next level or make a lateral shift to the next lane. Making a lateral shift like joining a new team, division or company at the same or higher level can speed up your career substantially too. You may get blocked again while in your new lane, but take it in your stride and work hard. If you see it is not working, then there is no one to stop you from changing your lane again.

An alert driver will always keep the front, side and rear view mirror in sight. Similarly, you need to be alert in sensing opportunities to ensure that you don't lose out any upcoming ones.

> *Always have a goal in your career. Be focused, be honest and work hard towards it. But also, be patient and understand that every hurdle you face in the path is a learning and is taking you closer to the goal.*
>
> ~GIRISH KAMATH, VICE PRESIDENT AND MANAGING DIRECTOR, INDIA, BALLY TECHNOLOGIES

3. SELF GOAL > ORGANIZATION GOAL?

A lot of people are frequently heard cribbing about their growth aspirations not having been met in a company and that their managers just doing lip service? Such complaints are not restricted to the average performer, but extend to high performers too. Have you ever wondered why? You have done everything that was possible, but your growth in the organization is still proving to be a challenge. This leads to frustration and losing trust in your manager. You start feeling stifled and totally demotivated and this can have an impact on your performance. This in turn, will make chances for your growth, dimmer. You enter a vicious circle.

Whenever you look for growth, think about what is good for you. You see a need to grab the position because you aspire for it. Such position is a logical extension of your career plan and you cannot imagine why the company should have an objection. You are so mired in your own world of thoughts that you stop thinking about what is good for the company.

What Can You Do?

If you want to grow in an organization, you need to understand your organization well. Although this may not be evident at junior levels, but as you grow, a lack of such understanding will hurt you. It could happen that the positions that you aspired for may be denied to you by the company. Organizations can choose to keep positions vacant instead of offering it to you. Hence, it is important to know the health and challenges of your organization to understand the rationale better. For senior positions, cost also becomes a factor in deciding to have such a position. Even the size of the organization also dictates the ratio of senior/middle management to employees, and therefore might not go for opening any new position or filling any vacant position, just because the organization size and ratio does not warrant it. If you sense an opportunity, you need to present it in a right way. By letting the management know that you can take on the responsibility in addition to your current responsibilities, without asking for a promotion or benefits, they might be more amenable about considering the request. If they see this flexibility in you, you are in a good place. Sometimes, if the role does not meet your expectations, go back to your previous role, but only after you have finished the assigned tasks and after informing the management of your reasons for withdrawing yourself from this additional responsibility.

If you are doubtful about your new position, keep your current role for some time keeping your manager in the loop. Only when convinced should you make the full transition to the new role. Once in the new role, start expanding the role and be patient. The organization will get a clear sense of your work soon and will promote you as soon as they are convinced that you deserve it.

In some cases, even if the management loves your idea and helps in shaping the new role, they may not offer you the role. Although you may be despondent about not getting the position, be satisfied that you were able to help the organization. Take it positively because your suggestion and help will not go unnoticed.

People rise by sensing opportunity, and creating opportunities for themselves provided they know their organization's needs well. Those who demand and ask for growth without keeping their organization needs in mind can sometime be lucky, but that is not a norm.

> *If you keep doing whatever you are doing, and do it well without expectations and putting in that extra bit with sincerity and passion, there is no way that your efforts and excellence will go unrecognized. Basically*

you have to enjoy whatever you are doing without any expectations and at the same time, if the need requires you to make your point, you can express yourself in a positive manner.

~IRFAN RAZACK, CHAIRMAN AND MANAGING
DIRECTOR, PRESTIGE ESTATES PROJECTS LIMITED

4. THE ETHICAL CONUNDRUM

It is natural for you to desire for a faster career growth. You have work hard, sometimes long hours, acquire new skills and try out many things to climb the organizational ladder faster. However, in the quest for faster growth, you choose to have just an office life. You are working or thinking all the time about work so that you don't miss any opportunities to rise. You want to be in limelight by being the first to reply to emails even at odd hours to get the tag of being available 24/7.

This could slowly start giving you returns as your manager starts depending on you. The rewards motivate you further to achieve more and more. Sometimes this vicious circle of performance and rewards leads to crossing the thin line of the ethical and non-ethical ways of doing business. Although all companies have an employee handbook describing the dos and don'ts, for example, sharing sensitive information, gift policy, financial submissions, entitlements as per career levels; sometimes you can form a process based on what you observe around you. If not vetted with the right stakeholders, this could land you on the wrong side and suddenly, from being the one who is never questioned, you may be catapulted into a situation where you need to justify your actions. All your smart working and networking, ever increasing responsibility and high visibility come to a naught. You may be caught totally off guard and start blaming your manager, organization and work environment for such a sudden break in your career. You will put all your energies into proving your innocence, and the result could be at best 50 per cent in your favour.

What Can You Do?

Respect your company policies and practices. Company policies are usually very well documented and accessible. However, it is understanding the practice that takes some time. Although most of the time, things could be okay. However you could get trapped because either you assumed a certain practice or a way of doing things, or you did not adhere to the written policy. Even if you have watched people doing things in a certain way, make sure that you know what the company policies are so that you don't just follow blindly, for when you are questioned, you will not have an answer. In such situations, whether knowingly or unknowingly, you will be in trouble. So it is better that you understand that you are an employee and every company has checks and balances in place. So curb your urge to close things in a hurry without due diligence. Even if they promise you tangible or non-tangible benefits, make sure that what you do is within the framework of the company policy. If in doubt, get it approved in writing from the right authority.

Sometimes you don't ask the right people for fear of sharing the credit. You do not want to reveal your connections with the customer/supplier/vendor or any external agency so as not to lose the exclusivity or because they feel it is premature, and thereby take the wrong steps. Always remember that you are an employee and that you need to protect yourself by working within the guidelines set by the company. In a hurry to clinch the deal and be the sole person to get accolades, some people go ahead and seal the deal without actually having the authority to do so. Avoid such greed.

There are other examples too. Sometimes, in the hurry to showcase a new product prototype, you may want to put forth products that have not been experimented on long enough and some data might be extrapolated which could easily be wrong, if the decision is made based on such parameters. Beware of this. Because when the truth comes out, you will be questioned.

If you are giving or receiving a gift, remember your company policy on it. Always make sure that you get a written approval for things that cost more, beforehand. Be careful of how you conduct yourself on business trips. Your evenings are partly covered by business, so if you do anything other than what you are supposed to, it will have a negative impact on you. Financial irregularities, taking/giving sexual favours, etc., are other examples. Stealing others' credit, where the other person can prove it, filing patents on your own and excluding your team members are other such things that will cast doubt on your integrity and honesty.

The second category is when you are fully aware of what you are doing. You only think of short-term gains and don't seem to be worried. As you grow in your career, these habits become hard to break. You could appear to be successful initially and might grow till mid level, but it will be difficult to grow further unless you change your habits.

The third category is when your manager has asked you to act in a certain way and later on, blames you for it. It will be in your best interest to get such a request in writing especially when you have a sense that this may not be the right request. Listen to your gut, check the policy and get the practice-related queries answered via email, and then decide whether to act or not. When in doubt, reach out to finance, HR, IT, vendor management team, etc., for clarity on the official practice or policy. Remember that no job is worth dying for. You simply escalate the issue and if you are still expected to do the job and do not want to, just quit. There are many examples of a whole team or sub-team being involved in unethical practice. If the company does not have a policy for whistle-blowers, it is better to quit if you feel very strongly about it.

> *The softest pillow is a clear conscience. That sometimes means when in Rome, don't do as Romans do.*
>
> ~MANISH SABHARWAL, CHAIRMAN,
> TEAMLEASE SERVICES

5. ARE YOU READY TO STEP UP?

You feel that promotion is your entitlement. You feel that since you have been loyal to the company for so many years and have clocked up so many years of experience, you are automatically qualified for the next level. It is almost like a right you have that the company has no other option but to promote you in order to retain you.

So if the promotion does not happen or even worse, if someone else gets promoted over you, all hell breaks loose.

Overnight, your manager becomes the villain. Slowly you start going into a shell and thinking more about what problem your manager has with you instead of the reasons for you not being promoted.

What Can You Do?

For a promotion, two things need to happen.

First, a business need for a position at a higher level. This need is determined on the current state of the organization, its potential growth, criticality, focus or the importance of such a position and some other factors. All these play a role in deciding whether such a position is needed, or even if there is a position that is open, whether there is a compelling reason to fill it up. This is normally not applied for junior positions.

The second criterion for promotion is whether a person is ready for the next level. This is where you have a control on your promotion. You need to prepare yourself for the next level much before you can expect a promotion. Never ask your manager 'When can I get promoted?' Instead, the right question is 'What skills do I need to demonstrate to move to the next level?' Sometimes, managers may not be prepared to give you an answer right away, but he will at least start thinking. He will be bound to answer you. You can help your manager to take a decision by presenting your case like 'I assume that you will be looking for a person to promote, and this is what I bring to the table'. This will show your manager that you have thought it through and are working towards it. Be ready to accept vague answers from him—and this will mainly be because he may not yet know till it will be discussed and decided in the right forum.

Once you get an idea on what is expected at the next level, you need to start demonstrating such traits and skills in your work—could be six months to a couple of years in advance. This will not only help strengthen your case, it will also help your manager to present your case to the forum.

You may think that you will acquire the skills after your promotion. You may also think that you may not be empowered to demonstrate such skills in your existing roles because you don't have such authority. There are many other reasons for not doing it at the current level. Remember, it is your career—therefore, the onus is on you to make an effort to move up, by asking, teaming up and by demonstrating. Unless there are visible signs of skills demonstrated for a level higher than your current one, your case for promotion will continue to be weak.

It is also important for you to be cognizant of the fact that it is not your manager or your manager's boss who are the only ones to decide your promotion. It is always a forum, and you should make an effort to find out who else is part of the forum. Some members of the forum might change when the actual meeting takes place, but usually the core group remains the same. Once you know who is in the forum, try building relationships with them. Subtly, let them know about your contributions and strengths. This will help immensely when your case is presented.

If you are denied a promotion, you have the right to ask your manager why this happened. Either he has not presented your case well or the forum is not convinced that you can do the job. This is why it is important to build relationships with them much before the final cut. When you make yourself visible to the forum, they are familiar with you and your contributions. Hence, they are likely to consider your case with full seriousness even if your manager's presentation is not good. Sometimes, a manager has the daunting task of choosing one among equals. Although he may have tried hard to create more positions to accommodate the equals, but it may not have worked and he is forced to choose only one to promote. Ask your manager for an honest answer. If you doubt his response, judge for yourself and act on what you think is important for you to develop further. Stay positive and try to reach out to the other members of the forum who could give you valuable inputs on what they want. It is equally important to update your manager on your areas of improvement that you have identified after listening and discussing with various stakeholders. You have the right to show displeasure, but do it professionally. How and how fast you bounce back from such setbacks never go unnoticed.

> *Know what is expected, but also walk the extra mile and always strive for world-class, even though nobody is watching.*
>
> ~GERD HOEFNER, MANAGING DIRECTOR AND CEO, SIEMENS TECHNOLOGY AND SERVICES PVT. LTD.

6. A MENTOR IS BETTER THAN A GODFATHER

When you are stuck in your career you dream of having a godfather who can provide the much-needed push.

Having a senior person in the company who takes care of your ambitions is great. Whenever he spots a new opportunity, he refers your name. He pushes for your promotion; he works out a deal with the management that gives you more visibility. Even when he leaves the company, his goodwill remains and that helps you immensely.

The desire to have such a godfather becomes stronger when you see a colleague or junior rising faster than you. He or she may not have any superior skills, but has risen because of his or her godfather.

It is quite easy to identify the person who rises in an organization very quickly. People talk behind his back saying that he has risen because of his godfather's help. Even if he is assigned a meaty assignment because he is competent, it is seen as the work of his godfather and becomes a subject of ridicule during breaks. The person could get slowly isolated by the others for fear of what he could be communicating upwards. As people like him grow some of them start forming their own power centre with people trying to get into his good books.

What Can You Do?

It is natural to expect that someone should help you in your career. But beware of wishing for a godfather. Without realizing it, sooner or later, your name will get associated with him and all your achievements will be contributed to him and not to you. You might find your colleagues passing snide remarks or taunting you. If you continue to take help from your so-called godfather, it is imperative that you will be obliged. And once your godfather asks for his pound of flesh, you will have to extend that support even if you feel that it is not right. This will bind you in an ethical dilemma. If your godfather is some levels higher than you, and over the years has been stuck at the same level while you grow, your relationship could take an ugly turn too. He might become competitive or vindictive and this sour relationship cannot be hidden.

Everyone needs mentors at different stages of their careers. Don't shy away from asking for advice. You can discuss anything from taking additional responsibility to exploring creative solutions to a given problem. You can brainstorm various possibilities if you are stuck at something. It all depends on your relationship with your mentor. You can also change the mentor depending upon the stage in your career and the value which your mentor will bring at that stage. In mentor-mentee relationship there is no expectation of reciprocity. It is safe and helpful to change when you feel you would be better off with another mentor because your existing mentor may not have anything more to offer. Always do it smoothly making sure that your relationship stays good with the earlier mentor.

It is not necessary that your mentor is within your company. You could have one outside the company. You could also have more than one mentor at a given time. Mentors provide perspectives which are beyond your work scope and might open up new horizons for you. It is important to have a network both within and outside your company. Networks provide an opportunity to identify mentor(s) and seek their help.

> *You need a mentor more than a godfather—to help you become what you can be in life instead of remaining what you are now.*
>
> ~BRIGADIER [RETD] K. HARIKUMAR, EXECUTIVE DIRECTOR, HYDERABAD SOFTWARE ENTERPRISES ASSOCIATION

7. YOU, THE BRAND

Most people are unaware of their own branding, and even if they are aware of it, they hardly put any effort into building it. Whether you like it or not, even without your knowledge or effort, a brand slowly starts building around you.

Have you been surprised when a position is denied and on enquiring you get a roundabout answer? Or you are denied an opportunity because they are looking for a specific skill that they feel you don't have? You could have that skill, but then if you are not branded, you are bypassed. How do you feel when you receive the same type of feedback from your manager year after year despite your continuous hard work? It is because once you are branded with particular traits, it takes time to notice the change. When they notice the change, they will first wait to see whether the change is permanent or not. Once they find that the change is permanent then, they will acknowledge it.

The sooner you realize that a brand is built around you, the better you will be equipped to mould it to a certain extent. How can you identify your brand? You can ask people with whom you interact the most and those who matter most in your career growth about what they see in you. You will easily know your characteristics by which points are repeated. That is your brand. If you have been labelled as aggressive, dynamic, but impatient and less tolerant, then that's your brand. If you don't like any of the adjectives, you need to work hard to change them. It could take months and sometimes, years to change them to what you want, but you need to persevere. Sometimes your basic nature may not support the new adjective with what you wish to be and therefore, it is important that you align it with what is natural to you. Your brand extends to your skills too. It is always a combination of your behavioural style and your domain knowledge.

Most organizations provide checkpoints for individuals to gauge the brand they are building for themselves. It happens during appraisal time when the manager reaches out to people you have interacted with to gather various perspectives about you. Sometimes an external consultant is roped in for a 360 degree feedback where the consultant meets team members, peers, managers and other stakeholders to find out details about you. The action does not stop here, consultants can work with the employee to choose a couple of areas of improvement and facilitate them with an action plan.

Is it important to be brand conscious? Why can't you just be what you are, and let others think what they want to think? You can take any stand, but then be prepared to face hurdles in your career growth, due to perceptions about you which you don't like. The better way is to be aware of your brand, and then decide whether you have to live with it or change it. Awareness is important.

What Can You Do?

Once you are aware that you have to build a brand to avoid people labelling you with an unwanted brand focus on building it. It is easier to develop and simpler to manage if your brand aligns with your natural traits. If you are aggressive, you cannot become docile even if you wish to. The brand consciousness will help to polish the aggressiveness to enable you to use it productively. You can choose to improve your strength further to dwarf your weakness or you can choose to improve a weakness that can help in removing the irritant in your way. Either way will help to refine your brand. Once you start paying attention to building your own brand, you will slowly start hearing positive comments like 'He has changed—for better!'

Your aptitude matters in brand building. Sometimes at middle and senior levels, it is difficult to distinguish individuals based on aptitude as they might be more or less similar. It is their behavioural skills that become the differentiator. Traits like attitude can blemish or enhance your brand. Attitude becomes visible in the very first interaction. One thing that helps in developing a positive attitude is to look for a silver lining in every failure. Optimism, enthusiasm and passion also help to build a positive attitude. But mere words are not sufficient. Actions should speak louder than words. The right action and positive attitude will help in building the right brand which leaves an everlasting impression.

Communicating clearly is another great trait that helps in branding. It helps others understand easily what you stand for. It is important to have an effective communication to avoid misunderstandings that could become serious. Crisp, clear and concise communication helps in avoiding controversies and reinforcing one's stand.

Some traits are non-negotiable for building a brand. Honesty is the most important of these. If you are dishonest, and don't care who you hurt to get what you want, people will tolerate you once or twice, but after that they will be cautious in dealing with you. Those who change their stance without acknowledging that they had an earlier stance might be considered non-trustworthy. Those who knowingly steal others' credits are seen as non-team players. Rumour-mongers are approached for the latest spicy news, but when the time for responsibility comes, they are often bypassed. So beware of how you behave in your workplace. All these negative traits can hurt your growth.

It is important to be able to admit to a mistake, say sorry, and sometimes, walk an extra mile to resolve a deadlock in professional relationship. These are some other traits that can help in building your brand.

> *The heart is brainier than the brain.*
>
> ~DHIRAJ RAJARAM, FOUNDER AND CEO, MU SIGMA

8. VISIBILITY MATTERS

Sometimes you are not visible within your own team or even to your own manager forget about a wider audience. You may complain about not being acknowledged in discussions and appraisals in spite of you having helped colleagues, taking up additional responsibilities or signing up for new initiatives. The manager is always blamed for not being aware of what is going on around him. But it is your responsibility to make his 'extra' work visible. You should be in control of your own career. If you cannot project yourself well, then even the manager will not be able to help you. You need to subtly beat your own drum without being pompous about it. Not only is being visible in your team a must, it is also important to be visible outside your immediate team. As you grow in the organization, you need to extend the reach of your visibility. Visibility does not mean that people know you only by name and face—they should be aware of some of your key skills.

You need to put some effort right from the beginning by ensuring that you have the right brand and extend the reach of visibility. A good test of visibility is to check if your name comes to decision makers' minds whenever a new opportunity comes up in the area where you have strength.

What Can You Do?

The best way to increase your visibility is to interact with more and more people, especially with those high in the hierarchy. Don't restrict yourself in your comfort zone, interacting with only the ones with whom your day-to-day tasks are dependent upon. Others do not want to take up visible assignments for the fear of failure. Taking up these types of projects will make you more visible to senior management. All customer-related issues are critical and highly visible too. Any simple additional efforts that can help the team, division or company can also give you great visibility. Initiatives like cost saving, increased productivity, shrinking timeline are the areas that can bring more visibility to you.

Look at networking within your organization. You need to understand the internal relations of your team first to develop your network with them. All organizations have multiple informal groups which network with each other and keep the grapevine alive by keeping an eye on whatever's happening in the company.

Other ways to make yourself visible are to team up with the go-getters and troubleshooters and work on visible projects and slowly try to become a go-getter or a troubleshooter yourself.

When you are in a circle of friends, you should be careful, as you can be labelled with that circle provided you want to be associated with that circle. Moving around with high performers who are already well known will also increase your visibility. Try not to be with the same sets of people all the time. Choose to spend your breaks with a new set of people each time to know what's happening around you.

Sometimes as you grow, you tend to spend more time with juniors, to guide, mentor or help them. Always remember that it is equally important to spend time with your seniors. By doing this, you will be aware of the challenges being faced at the senior level and be prepared for it. The message is to balance your interactions with all levels to get a holistic view of the pulse of the group, division or organization.

Try and volunteer for projects that give you a chance to interact with new people and senior management. Representing your team or division in internal or external events also adds to your visibility. Try and be part of activity groups that involve people across teams. Send emails to a wider audience about something significant—this will add to your recognition.

> *You need to take your destiny in your own hands to be a successful leader. Get to know your personal brand, and do everything necessary to make it.*
>
> ~SRINIVAS PRASAD, CEO—PHILIPS INNOVATION CAMPUS, BENGALURU

9. BE NETWORKED

There is no doubt that networking within your industry is a great way to grow. Everyone agrees with this, but few make an effort to do so.

Networking has become easier as so many social media and other internet platforms are available. Although these can help to increase your connections, a large number of connections may not always translate into actual networking. Actual networking means a good understanding between people. They need to have a rapport—such that you can reach out to others without inhibitions. Networking can start with an introductory email, but then needs to be nurtured and kept alive.

Why do you need to make an extra effort to network? If you are a networked person you are a great asset to your company because you have so much information—whether it is about your competitors or customers or suppliers. Your contacts will naturally lead you to have a good knowledge of organization structure, type of projects and a rough compensation prevalent in the industry. This gives you an edge in the company. You will be not only respected but also greatly sought after for market intelligence or for referrals. If you are a well-networked employee, you will be armed with information and this will help you to discuss confidently with your manager about what you are looking for. And if you are a well-networked manager be sure that your employees will know that they cannot take you for a ride.

Being well-networked also acts like a safeguard for you within the organization because people will think twice before rubbing you the wrong way.

The benefits are manifold. A well-networked entrepreneur can find a suitable venture capitalist; a professional can find a trusted mentor; a student can make the right choice to get the right employer; a senior executive can find an effective organizational coach, and so on. In this uncertain and unstable business world, networking provides some fallback and gives mental peace.

What Can You Do?

Simply dreaming about having an extensive network in the industry might not work, you need to actively pursue it. But, how to network? You can join a golf, soccer or bridge club if your interest matches these. You can also attend networking dinners of alumni and entrepreneurship associations or join a marathon, biking or drama group. These not only provide a fertile ground for meeting and exchanging ideas, but also could be the beginning of some great partnerships. Another thing you can do is to start or join a domain-based interest group, for example, any new technology, new consumer product, new quality standard, new process, etc. It is not enough to just join an association of interest, you need to make an effort to periodically attend the meets so that you are not forgotten.

What happens when two strangers meet? The first thing they do is to find a common point between them. This icebreaker could be anything—from the geography they belong to the educational institutes they attended, companies they worked with, associations they belong to, languages they speak, political inclinations, common people or a common hobby. This helps to get into a comfort zone. Over time, topics like professional growth and career opportunities are also discussed. Breaking the ice is easy for those who have mastered the art of good conversation.

Are you the type who hesitates to start a conversation with a stranger? If you want to widen your network then you need to start honing this skill. All relationships have to be 'mutually beneficial'. This is controversial because you may associate the word 'beneficial' with the material world. Here, it means a meaningful interaction that can help both parties. Have you noticed how the initial hype during a first interaction slowly fades away? Even when you promise to meet again, such meetings usually don't take place. This is because both parties do not get the results they expect. Sometimes, you could be keen to meet, but the other person might not be interested in continuing because it doesn't interest him enough. However, all is not lost. Even one-time interactions can help you to increase your awareness of that section of society or industry. It also helps you to sharpen your communication skills when you are not in your comfort zone.

The 'beneficial' could also be just a good feeling, i.e., you may feel good talking to the other person even though both of you have nothing in common. You need to understand that you also need to offer something interesting to the other person. Here your art of conversation, together with your expanse of knowledge will help to bond better. So look at yourself first and gauge what you can offer, and then, only then, see what others offer.

Technology has bridged the gap among people. Whether it is through a cellphone or a computer or a tab, you can connect with anyone anywhere at any time. However, in spite of all these technological advancements, the best form of networking is still face-to-face interaction, at least initially. This type of interaction provides a high comfort level where you know that conversations cannot be recorded, and therefore, cannot be used against you in the future even if the relationship turns sour. And most importantly, it shows human emotions, which are more powerful than words. However, to have such interactions, you need to find the time to meet and this could require travel also.

Many organizations provide avenues to expand your network. You can join groups within organizations and represent your company in various events, competitions in the industry, or volunteer for some social service and thus network with others. You can also become an office bearer of interest groups like book reading clubs, toastmasters, quiz clubs, etc., and invite external teams, experts or speakers, which again, is a good way to network.

> *Business is all about networking. Networking within an organization and outside the organization is critical for success. Networking with customers, investors, press, vendors and industry bodies help in strengthening a company visibility and build business.*
>
> ~B.V.R. MOHAN REDDY, FOUNDER AND EXECUTIVE
> CHAIRMAN, CYIENT

10. MR HIGH MAINTENANCE

Have you ever thought about what your manager thinks about your never-ending demands? Of course, you must speak your mind and state clearly what you are looking for. Not doing so can have a serious impact on your career. But, have you judged the frequency of your requests? Your request could be anything: some work of your liking, a review of compensation, transfer to another location, change of team, asking when you will be promoted, and so on. There is nothing wrong in asking, but sometimes people keep demanding things in quick succession. Once one demand is met, they make their next demand within no time. A manager's job is to align each individual's goals with the organizational goal. He has a large number of people to look after and if they all make demands in quick succession; it is difficult for him to manage the situation. Meaty opportunities are always limited and the manager needs to divide them fairly. Certainly, high performers might get a bigger chunk, but it will not always be every time. You may believe that you are not getting what you deserve and therefore keep asking for the same thing by modifying it to appear a new request. It is imperative to understand that each new request adds up in your manager's mind. This could lead to frustration and when your manager feels that he cannot handle it any further, he takes up the issue with *his* manager. It is highly likely that your manager will slowly start moving you out from the criticality. This is true even for a high performer who may be considered as a high maintenance person and is added to a 'don't care' list of employees.

What Can You Do?

To avoid falling into a situation of being labelled with such a tag, be aware of what you are asking for and how important such a request is for you. Try not to get influenced by your peers' wishes and analyze what it is that you really want. If you are in a dilemma and don't know how to proceed, speak to your manager directly to help you to resolve it. But, pose the question as a dilemma and work on his suggestions. This will not be considered a demand as it's a manager's job to help you in such situations. It is true that you may have your own timeline and sometimes your personal circumstances may force you to ask for such requests in a hurry to align a narrow window of opportunity. If so, explain the situation to your manager.

When you are absolutely certain that this is what you really want, place your request to your manager either as an exploratory option or as your immediate need. In both cases, do provide the perspective of your request. This will not only show honesty, but also that you have done a thorough research and are serious about it. Your manager could respond immediately or buy some time. So far so good. But here's where your art of conversation comes into play, i.e., how are you asking?

The way you ask, the words you use and your body language speak too. Some people's body language shows that it is their birth right to get such demands fulfilled, while others' tones appear to be a veiled threat of quitting. There are some who won't budge without knowing the timeline and some who are so shaky and apologetic in asking that it shifts the focus from the real issue to something else. Try and have a conversation in such a way that you show that the manager is also part of your decision making.

> *Understanding the holistic impact of the ask and having an open discussion with the manager is a good approach.*
>
> ~PRADEEP DESAI, EX-GE GLOBAL RESEARCH,
> TECHNOLOGY LEADER, SOFTWARE SCIENCES &
> ANALYTICS–INDIA

11. GROOMING QUOTIENT

Imagine that you are part of an interview panel. What is the first thing you notice about a candidate who walks in? Your eyes will scan the person's attire and personal grooming. You may be unconscious of this fact as your eyes and brain are so tuned to coordinate this, but it is a fact that the first image of a person sticks in your mind, at least for some time. So when you do this to others, why don't you look at yourself in the mirror and judge how you yourself are dressed for office.

Today, not all jobs require formal dressing at work. But it is very important for those who deal with customers or external stakeholders to be dressed formally and be presentable. Some organizations have a dress code and that makes it easy. For the majority that does not have one, it becomes a little dicey. In such cases, the onus lies on the employee to dress as per the company culture. What is the harm if sports shoes give way to formal shoes, casual round neck t-shirts get replaced by shirts at least for a few days in the week and non-office bags should be switched to office bags.

Personal grooming plays a huge role too. Meetings, one-on-one discussions, brainstorming sessions and other interactions at work require co-workers to be in close proximity to each other. Wearing clean clothes and maintaining good personal hygiene make working together pleasant. Not doing above, could hinder interactions at work and impact not only the project progress, but also impact your brand.

Why are such things important inside an office?

Just as you form an opinion of a candidate, your attire adds to your personality and one's opinion of you. Whenever your name is discussed for a new role or responsibility, you may be turned down. Although none of the members usually point out such things, they can vaguely say that your style, attitude or approach will not be suitable for that opportunity. Dressing well and personal grooming are easy things to change, so why let them come in way of your career growth?

What Can You Do?

Some organizations have a written dress code policy. If your organization has one, then simply follow it. Most organizations do not specify a dress code, but simply state what should be avoided, for example, sleeveless tops, collarless t-shirts, shorts, etc., while others simply state that Friday is the day for casual dressing. It is therefore up to you to make changes in your dressing that can help you. If you want to grow to manage a team or increase your sphere of influence to interact with a wider audience and sometimes across countries, you need to come across as a person who is well-groomed and in control of himself. You need not always be dressed in expensive and fashionable garments, but your appearance should reflect that you take care of yourself. Take five minutes extra every morning to ensure that you have a clean and fresh look.

You cannot change how you look, but you can at least

dress appropriately to enhance your personality. Start making a change in your wardrobe. Don't worry about jokes or remarks from co-workers. Such situations will disappear after a while. Your colleagues and friends will get used to it and slowly your personal image will also start changing. Your manager and others who matter will certainly notice it.

Personal hygiene and grooming also play a huge role in your career growth. By the time they start the job, most people have already formed a grooming schedule for themselves. Make sure you shave quite frequently if not daily. If you sport a beard or moustache, maintain it well. Being unshaven, having body odour, wearing crumpled clothes and having dirty or unkempt hair are some of the major put-offs. As you grow older, your body needs change. Hence, the grooming schedule of your college days might not help you. You need to adapt with time.

A lot of managers who themselves are very finicky give a lot of weightage to such things because they believe that 'if a person cannot take care of himself, how can he take care of higher responsibilities. If he does not have time for himself, how can he find time to deal with the challenges in his new role?'

You might wonder why all this should matter at work. After all, to carry out the job entrusted to you, only your skills matter. Taking the example of the candidate at an interview again—remember how you gauged his knowledge, capabilities and other skills? Was it not after your first impression of how he was groomed and dressed? Doesn't final impression about him takes everything into account?

It is a similar case with your manager too. He may be

very familiar with your skills but your attire and grooming also play a part in his impression of you. So do take personal grooming more seriously and see how your own self-esteem increases too.

> *I think everyone feels it's a good thing, but we sometimes take it easy. Attire and personal grooming surely play a big role.*
>
> ~YUKIO TAKEYARI, MANAGING DIRECTOR, SONY INDIA
> SOFTWARE CENTRE PVT. LTD

CHAPTER TWO

MANAGING YOUR MANAGER

12. THE MAN FRIDAY

Like Robinson Crusoe every manager wants to have his own Friday. If there is more than one man Friday in the team, the manager is lucky. It is up to the manager to provide an environment that can facilitate the conversion of a person to become a man Friday. Such people can do anything for the manager and for the company. They can be trusted under any extreme circumstances and help in coming out of crisis. They are not yes men but are considered dependable. They can think of fresh ideas, new suggestions, out-of-box solutions to problems and can handle a tense situation easily. They provide unquestionable support.

What Can You Do?

Here are some qualities that can make you a man Friday.

Be Ethical, Honest And Dependable: Ethics are fundamental

to any relationship. Strive to be ethical in whatever you do. When in doubt, seek advice from your boss or other senior stakeholders. Never steal others' credit, always share it if working in a team. Honesty is always rewarded and leaves a positive lingering impression. Admit to your mistakes and never hesitate to break the news, whether bad or good. When people around you know what you stand for, they will always look for you to discuss issues, seek advice and sometimes, ask for help. Do what you have promised to do to earn the title of being dependable.

Be a Problem Solver And Flexible: Be realistic in raising an issue, but try to provide a solution to resolve it. Develop an attitude of a go-getter and find a silver lining in all problems are those who managers approach the most. Managers are paid salaries not just to find solutions to problems, but they are responsible for their execution too. A manager could be the decision maker but finding the solution is a team effort and therefore get involved in trying to find solutions.

At any given time in any company, there are multiple projects running at different stages. Some could be at an investigation stage, while others are entering a high-risk category, while others are nearing completion and do not require much attention. In addition to this, there could be more twists and turns like real-time change of scope or direction or even the purpose of a project. A manager's job is to juggle his people between the projects so as to successfully complete the work on time smoothly. Managers therefore tend to reach out to employees who are flexible in their work assignments and help in realizing the team goals. So be flexible in your thoughts and learn to adapt to new situations quickly so that you are in the frontline when your manager wants to assign a new job. Flexibility provides an edge during performance appraisal too.

Develop Good Communication And Interpersonal Skills: A winning team has members with good interpersonal skills and mutual trust and respect for each other. They could have many disagreements and may not be receptive to others occasionally, but they handle it adroitly. They form a strong bond due to their good interpersonal skills. There could be outbursts, heated discussions, accusations or even trust issues, but then you can overcome these by reaching out to others. Developing good interpersonal skills is a good way to get along and understand your team members. It helps to form strong bonds with them. By forming strong bonds, you learn to understand and appreciate another person's point of view without spoiling relationships. This skill is not only useful for work but also in your personal life.

The requirement of having good communication skills is more acute in a large team. Miscommunication or the lack of proper communication can not only lead to a complete failure of a project but also spoil the teaming.

Have Subject Matter Knowledge: Having subject matter knowledge is very important for you to survive and grow in an organization. It is normally said that in medical or legal professions, a person will fall by the wayside if he is not in touch with the latest developments in his field. But this is true for almost every field today. To survive the cut-throat world of today, you need to spend time in refining your skills, understanding new trends and researching your area of work. Keeping abreast of the latest techniques will stand you in good stead, not only with your colleagues, but also with your managers. All managers acknowledge and respect people who bring in new ideas and suggestions on doing things in a better way.

You may have many excuses for not upgrading your skills. Don't blame your manager for overloading you with work and thus leaving you with no time to read or do anything else, or for not organizing training courses. Don't forget that your skill improvement is your responsibility. Organizations provide training that is required from their perspective, but putting an onus on the organization or the manager for individual skill improvement is the first sign of failure of a person. Very few people spend their own money to sharpen their skills or by reading or trying out something new. Try and squeeze out as much time as you can from your busy schedule as that will make you highly desirable and much sought by managers.

Be Hardworking And Ask For More Work: You should be hungry for work and ask for more work. All good managers love employees who keep asking for more work. However, before asking for more work, make sure that you have completed all previously assigned work. Sometimes, managers do not assign additional work for other reasons. These could range from seeing that employee does not have enough bandwidth to take up additional work, or when the current work requires more focus. It could also be that others have shown interest earlier or are better qualified to take on the assignments. If you face such a situation, spend some time in sharpening your skills, discussing, brainstorming or informally interacting with other team members to learn.

You may feel that there is no point in repeatedly asking for more work because you will not get it since it has been denied to you multiple times in the past. The advantage in publishing your available bandwidth is to ensure that your manager does not make statements like, 'You've done just what you've been asked to do'. This will not only deny him an opportunity to put the onus on you during your performance review, but he will be more specific in giving feedback in this area to you. But an even better approach is that you try and experiment with things that interest your team to sharpen your own skills, rather than waiting for the manager to give you something. This will show your manager that you are a no-nonsense person and value your own time. Sooner or later, your manager will be bound to consider your request.

It may be difficult to get all these qualities in one person, but honing even few of these qualities can make you a good man Friday.

> *An early piece of career advice given to me: Look at what your manager does and seek to off-load as much as you can from your manager. I see this as a common trait in high-performers. It helps one learn and grow rapidly since one begins to take on responsibilities far beyond what's expected of them. Career trajectories similarly reflect this higher impact. The tip to be your manager's man Friday deeply resonates and is a key ingredient for success.*
>
> ~KIRTHIGA REDDY, MD, FACEBOOK INDIA

13. WINNING YOUR MANAGER

Winning over any boss is a tough challenge. Most of the time you don't know what he really wants. You may struggle to find out what makes your manager happy or you may end up doing something stupid while trying, and thus fall further in the eyes of your manager. Finally, after a few unsuccessful tries, you give up and resign yourself to your fate.

What Can You Do?

Here are some tips that could help you to win over your manager if done in the right way.

Praise/Acknowledge the Boss When He Deserves It: A boss is also human and wants to be praised and appreciated. Genuine praise carries huge value. Even a simple thank you to the boss for resolving a tough issue will be sufficient. Fine-tune the frequency of praise based on the nature of your boss, as doing it too often could dilute the importance and make you seem like a sycophant. Make sure that it is appropriate for the occasion. When your team members praise your manager in front of his peers, he could sometimes be ridiculed for sucking up to the boss. However, when the praise is deserved, there is no harm in acknowledging and wishing him in public. In fact, your peers will look at it in a positive way and will, in all probability, join you too!

Provide an Early Warning To Your Boss: It is sensible to alert your boss when his actions or decisions impact one or more team members. But beware of becoming an informer or mole because that could alienate you from your team. Approach your manager as a responsible team member and provide your perspective. Speak with others of your team and find out if it is bothering them too. If yes, then you can go as team to your manager or inform them that you have already had such a discussion with your manager. If it is a common issue, a heads up to the manager is good, rather than raising it suddenly at a meeting and surprising your manager.

If you attend a meeting where your boss is not present and you sense that a decision that could impact your team or him adversely is being taken, request that your boss be involved in the decision making. Else, equip your boss by informing him of the potential fallout along with any suggestions you may have.

Support Your Supervisor In Meeting His Goals And Help Him To Rectify His Mistakes: Don't just do what is assigned to you. Keep your boss updated and seek help only when required. He could be struggling with many issues: these could be speed breakers in a project or a threat from competition, or even a missed deadline thrown as a challenge to him. A manager may not open up immediately if you ask him, but if he feels that you are genuinely concerned, he will open up and ask you for suggestions or solutions, even if he ultimately does not agree with your suggestions, he will know that you are concerned. Such attitude and thinking beyond the assigned task will always help you in your career growth.

What happens when your boss informs you of a surprising decision taken by the management? Can you stand up and tell your boss that the decision is erroneous or will you talk behind his back and criticize him?

It is important to point out the challenges in implementing such a decision. If your manager is open, well and good, but if he is closed, then don't take it further because you have no option but to implement the decision. Sometimes he could have committed to something under pressure from his management or customers just to save the situation without thinking about how it would be done or whether it could be done at all. Have you ever come forward to save your boss from a bad decision? Did you do your best to rectify it so that he is not embarrassed in front of others for having taken a bad call? Those who come forward and pull out their bosses from a quagmire are the smart ones and are sure to be noticed, remembered and rewarded suitably.

Some bosses may take the help but will not acknowledge or give credit for it. Don't be discouraged by this. Treat it as an opportunity for knowing what your boss is really like under such circumstances. To get credit, some employees start speaking to a wider audience about how they helped their boss—never do that—it could damage your case further. Just continue to be helpful. Even if your boss doesn't acknowledge you in public, he will know. And if you continue to take a positive approach and approached again for help, sooner or later the management and others who matter to you will also come to know. So be patient and continue the good work.

Cover Your Supervisor's Weak Points: Every person has weak points and so does your supervisor. If his presentation skills are weak, suggest that he splits the presentation into separate sections and let others people speak about their respective sections. If your supervisor cannot handle complex people issues, suggest solutions and ideas. If he is not a subject matter expert and does not understand finer details, help him out with points and presentations so that he can put his points forward in a discussion with his boss. Extend your support to your boss in whichever way you can and see how far it will take you.

A word of caution: sometimes a boss could recognize his weak areas, but may not want to make it public for fear of exposing his own shortcomings. While some ask for help explicitly, most try to ask for it surreptitiously to hide their own weaknesses. So beware of how you offer your help. Choose the right approach and see how far you can go.

> *This tip gives us how to get along with the manager, and also some learning to play the role of a manager yourself.*
>
> ~MASAYOSHI TAMURA, GM OF SOFTWARE GROUP, HITACHI INDIA PVT. LTD AND CO-CHAIR OF JAPAN COUNCIL, NASSCOM

14. UNDERSTANDING YOUR MANAGER

It is difficult to slot managers into categories. It is not true that your manager will not change in due course of time. Hence, it is better to view the following classifications from a broad perspective rather than on the basis of a few incidences. This is an attempt to understand a few strong traits displayed by a manager and how to handle them. It is possible that your manager may fall into multiple categories.

A Weak Supervisor

You wish for a weak boss so that you get the maximum freedom to do what you want to do. Although on the face of it, it sounds good, you should understand that a weak boss is neither good for the team nor for the organization. A weak boss will be seen with a lower dignity and that impression becomes applicable to the whole team. Sometimes because of his weak image, all important and challenging work will go to other teams. A weak manager may not be able to demand the right budget for employees' compensation and benefits either. He is in this position because he was a good performer once or had some subject skills in the past which have now become obsolete. Over time, he will fall further because he will not be able to keep track of his own skills with the changing priorities of the company and dynamic market.

An easy way to handle this type of a boss is to change your team. But this may not always be possible. If you have just joined the team, you may need to learn a lot more in the current assignment or learn how to handle the political environment without messing it up further. Whatever be your reason to stick around, you will need to work hard and make your contributions visible not only within the team but also outside the team, with little help from your manager. This will help you to build your own image instead of being adversely affected due to your manager's poor one.

There is also an advantage in working with this type of boss. He could be fired, transferred to a lower key position, or he could move on. If the management sees a smart employee with the right kind of visibility inside and outside the team with the right skills, he may get the opportunity to lead the team. If you are ready and the signals from the management make it clear that you are ready for the next level, then be patient and wait for your opportunity.

However, you cannot plan your career based on your manager's exit. So, if you get a lateral opportunity for growth that is in line with your career plan, go ahead and take it.

A Strong Supervisor

A strong supervisor is one who has fixed notions and could sometimes be dictatorial. He will make sure that everyone under him feels secure because he can handle external problems and resolve people management issues with ease through negotiations, and sometimes through coercion or fear. He will appear to be democratic but have strong ideas on everything and wants everything to be done exactly the way he wants it done. This is good, but not always a happy situation. His micromanagement could cause frustration and people may have to think twice before approaching him. If they do not approach him with full preparation, the meeting will be unproductive. Normally these types of people are high performers and extremely sharp. If convinced, they will go all out for all activities related to work or employee benefits. However convincing him takes time and requires good preparation from employees.

The best way to work with such managers is to be on top of things. Never hide any facts and if you don't know about something, ask for it rather than concealing it. Mentally prepare yourself with the questions he can ask and your probable answers. He has little tolerance for mistakes so be open in what you do and also be upfront with any mistakes you may have made. You can also learn a lot from him provided you focus on his strengths rather than thinking about how he talks and why he breathes down your neck.

A Facilitator Supervisor

This type of person does not have any inhibitions and is free for all. He grooms his team members and gives them enough freedom to take decisions and is tolerant about mistakes. He may not know each and everything that is happening within the team, but will keep an eye on the important ones.

This type of boss lets everyone define their own scope of work, take challenges based on their own skills to deliver results. He provides support whenever anyone needs it. Even when he is not convinced about someone's approach in solving a problem, he will give him a fair chance. Such a supervisor will coach his people, raise the bar and provide valuable feedback.

It is very easy to work with this type of boss. Being passionate about spending time to look ahead and therefore preparing the team for the future, he will delegate the day-to-day mundane, tactical work to his team members without interference, leading to higher empowerment. Although there is no apparent disadvantage with such a supervisor, some team members could be stressed about this type of management and style as empowerment leads to accountability. Unlike a 'strong supervisor' where he will own the decision and its consequences, this type of boss will hold the person responsible for any failures. Sometimes, such bosses are so hands-off that they may not be able to provide you with concrete advice.

The best way to handle such bosses is to keep them in

the loop about whatever is happening and seek their buy-in all decisions. Rather than shouldering the entire burden, it is better to seek their help in facilitating a resolution of thorny issues with difficult colleagues or other teams. Since he is good in facilitating things, he could easily do it for you, provided you have first tried and did not succeed.

Protector And Possessive Supervisor

Also called big daddy supervisor, this type of boss will take good care of you. However, if you ever try to be adventurous or show a desire to work on your own, you will be subjected to lots of obstacles. The advantage of having this type of boss is that he will shoulder all the problems provided he is fully informed about them. He'll insist on making the 'right' decisions for you even when you can easily tackle it. This hinders team members because they fail to develop their own skills due to their high level of dependency. Any mistake in the project or any issue within the team must be kept secret, and if any dissenting voice goes out, he will not be kind with the person doing it. Anyone with an average skill can easily survive well under such bosses, if he follows his basic tenets. Such bosses build an opaque team and are prone to be surrounded by yes men. If you are the type who argues and disagrees, or one who looks for alternative approaches and keeps emerging trends in mind, it will be a challenge to work under such a boss.

The best way to handle the situation is to surrender to him and agree to his decisions after voicing your concern. Keep mum even if your suggestions are not entertained. Try and build a relationship with him to understand his position on various topics so that you can align with him for good. Such bosses could be quite political too, so don't do anything that could weaken his position.

An Over-demanding Supervisor

This type of boss is a workaholic and difficult to please. At best he will be satisfied with the work but hardly be happy. He will raise the bar quite frequently and challenge his team to find better solutions. One should forget about getting any type of appreciation from him and be happy if he is not angry. The good thing about working with such a manager is that you will become rugged and will not shy away from any hard work or challenges in the future. Such a type of boss is also very good mentor and people who are hungry to learn and perform will be lucky to be groomed by him.

The best way to handle this type of manager is to agree to a common set of goals and also the ways to reach the goals. Whenever he is changing the goal or the process, make sure that you understand what is required from you and get it in writing otherwise he will think that you own the task, and a misunderstanding will crop up. It is important to ask for help on time so that any delays in the project do not prove costly for you. This type of manager will test your patience, sharpen your skills and make you aware of your limitations, all of which if taken in the right spirit, will help in your self-improvement immensely.

A Hierarchical Supervisor

This type of manager's interaction style, tone, responsiveness is all based on the position you occupy. You will notice the sudden change in his style when he is interacting with his team members and his senior manager drops by. His 'bossy' style quickly changes gears to a mild demeanour. He is the king and his team members are his subjects. He follows a strict hierarchy and in matrix management, listens only to those who are at a level higher to him or those who matter for his growth. Skip level dialogues do not exist in his dictionary. He assumes full authority as he knows that his team members will hardly reach out to his boss for any complaint. This becomes a disadvantage for this management style, as the team might work in silos and outside team level issue resolutions are usually very low as it has to go through the supervisor.

The best way to handle a hierarchical boss is to make him feel respected because of the position he enjoys. Be formal in your communication till he opens up on his own. Use the proper channel to escalate issues. Always make sure that you use the right mailing list—people who should be in 'To' list and who should be in 'CC' list are extremely important.

> *This tip has identified different personality traits of managers and explained very succinctly on how to manage such managers for your own success.*
>
> ~PRANESH ANTHAPUR, CHIEF PEOPLE OFFICE, NUTANIX

15. TUNING INTO YOUR MANAGER'S FREQUENCY

Do you wonder why your manager looks at certain issues in a particular way? Why he reacts in a way, which according to you is inappropriate for the situation? You are upset when such a reaction impacts you. This is because you have not understood your boss well. He has some inherent traits, which even if he tries to overcome, shows up sometimes. Understanding such traits will help you to understand your manager, and once you understand, you will find it is easier to tune yourself to it.

An Image-conscious Supervisor

This type of person is very friendly. He gets along well with everyone and is quite conscious about his own image. He does not like any controversies at the workplace and will work towards their resolution before they can happen. He is very social and expects people to praise his actions. He will try to take popular decisions and provide the background of any unpopular decision, if he is forced to take one.

It is easy to work with this type of boss as he is very transparent and open. Such bosses usually have memberships to associations or organizations and have a large circle of contacts in the industry. Build your bridges with him to be able to take his help in reaching out to.

Such a boss will take umbrage if because of your action or words his image takes a hit. If you are in disagreement, sort it out in private. If you feel the meeting will be controversial and appear to undermine your manager, it is better that you let him know before the meeting, and then take a stand.

A Miserly Supervisor

Every good supervisor should adhere to the allocated budget and should be frugal in spending. But some of them go beyond the definition of being frugal and become misers! This habit is evident in their everyday dealings where they are always focusing on cost-cutting even if there is no such directive from his management. On one hand, it is good that they are managing their team budgets with an iron fist, but on the other hand, this could cause huge dissatisfaction among his employees, as the same yardstick is not consistently followed in the other teams. Employees feel the pinch when it is about their team lunches, team-building exercises, travels, awards, bonuses and also to an extent, their pay hikes. Such bosses tend to question all invoices or vouchers submitted, so make sure that you put in all details of all expenditure.

What happens when you realize that your compensation and benefits are always a shade lighter than what you could have got under a different manager? The answer is there is nothing you can do about it. If you are unhappy, you could ask for a one-on-one discussion, but don't expect any major changes. By nature, these bosses are those who always give a little less. That little bit will hurt you, but not bite you.

Sometimes this miserly habit starts hindering a project because of the delays in approval leading to a delay in the ordering of things. In project-specific cases, it is therefore smart to mention the risks and timelines to your manager. Then, leave it to him to negotiate with vendors because he will get you the best price.

A Jealous Supervisor

It can be a very ugly situation when the supervisor becomes jealous of his own team members. But it happens. Your manager could be jealous of you for anything: you have better skills, you are more visible to the top management, you are approached for your opinions on critical issues, and so on. If you have made yourself a brand in the company and your manager has joined the company after you, this trait of jealousy will take over. If this trait is apparent, then avoid situations that could activate it. While a few managers are good actors in hiding their feelings, dealing with it might be difficult. Ideally, managers could leverage a lot from having such employees. But they are insecure as they feel that they could be destabilized from their position, job or ambition. Such people could be vindictive too so it's a good idea to stop boasting in front of them. Of course, you must highlight your work, but avoid discussing other achievements which are not directly related to the topic. Even if you are praised or appreciated by others, don't share it with your manager. If you feel suffocated, look for a change by reaching out to your manager's boss for suggestions and guidance.

But what happens when such a jealous manager is also a high performer? In that case it is better to understand him, learn from him what you lack and avoid situations that aggravate his jealousy. Over time you and your manager will be able to reach some type of balance in your relationship as you both will need each other. It could also be that you feel that he is jealous, but in reality he might not be so. He could just be targeting your blind spots and want you to realize it. He could be pointing out your shortcomings in your proposals and you could feel that he is jealous of your ideas. Talk with him openly to understand his perspective before you conclude that he is jealous of you.

A Selfish Supervisor

A selfish supervisor's primary motive is to look after himself. He will take care of his team to ensure that it helps him more than it helps the team. He will spend more time in self-promotion rather than guiding and grooming his team members. He will first see how he can hog the limelight even at the expense of his team members. The advantage of this type of manager is that being an attention seeker, he gets involved in high-profile activities making sure that good projects come to his team.

The disadvantage of having a manager like this is that he will help his team only if he sees that there is something good in it for him. He will always put himself first for awards or accolades and grab activities that will provide him visibility. The best way to handle such a supervisor is to feed him with new ideas and thoughts—those that you want to use for your own learning and growth. Make him aware indirectly that such initiatives will serve his career growth. Certainly he will present it as his own to his management, but once approved, he will ask you to work on it, and that is what you wanted in the first place! Slowly, he will start seeing value in you and once he feels that he can benefit much more by keeping you in his team, he will take care of you.

A Sadistic Supervisor

It happens ever so often that just when you have packed up and are about to leave for the day, your manager assigns you some work that needs to be finished immediately. Does your manager come late to work and stay late and expect you to be around till he's in office, even if it does not meet your schedule? Does he sit on your application for leave and not approve it till the last moment? Does he ask you to make last-minute change to your project report or presentation turned in well in advance? Such a kind of boss also places obstacles in your exit from the company after you have put down your papers. There are numerous such examples where you find managers showing their sadistic traits. Most of the time they do it out of habit, but on some occasions it is just to assert themselves.

It is difficult to handle this type of manager. Either you learn to live with them, or you leave. Know what to expect from them and be prepared to handle it. If you see that everyone in your team is going through the same ordeal, then console yourself that you are not the only target! Ignore some of the actions and you will be able to work peacefully. If you cannot tolerate it, and it is impacting your working life adversely, ask for change of team or leave the company.

An Aloof Supervisor

This type of manager can be called a distant supervisor. His interactions with his team are low, communication is to the point and he does not make any effort to bond. He sits in his office or cubicle most of the time. He is neither a cheerleader nor a motivator and usually tries to solve a problem on his own without even thinking of delegating or looking at what his team is doing.

Such a manager could be in that management role by mistake. He could be a high performer in his core area but he is not cut out to be a manager. He is usually a serious thinker who enjoys working in isolation, and this continues even when he is forced to take up management roles. He cannot understand or anticipate the warning signals of issues brewing in his teams. When he finally comes to know about it, he chooses to be a firefighting mode. Being minimally communicative, he won't get even a whiff of interpersonal issues within their own team and this could have a negative impact.

There is only one way to manage this type of a manager— go into his office, discuss the issue and get it resolved then and there. Use your communication skills and be proactive in involving the manager in decisions that require his attention. Learn from his expertise areas and slowly you will learn to be independent in doing things.

A Timekeeper Supervisor

Such type of a manager is highly self-disciplined and you can learn the importance of time from him. His meetings run on time and people need to come prepared for such meetings to save time. If you have committed to a date, you'd do well to stick to it. If you are running late, be sure you have a valid reason for it and have informed him well in advance. He does not like to waste time on less important, irrelevant things and expect the same from his team members too. He follows a highly disciplined routine in his daily life. Such a manager might be willing to settle for an acceptable 'little lower' quality output if it meets the requirement of a timely response. If you are a perfectionist, be prepared for a rude shock as time is paramount. This type of manager will not have unlimited time or patience for perfection. Although he expects perfection, he just wants things to happen within the stipulated time if it meets the requirement and is near perfect. He will get frustrated, if he is dependent on something or someone not under his control, if it impacts his own commitment.

Whether or not you are like him, such a manager will make sure that you adhere to a schedule. He respects his time and will respect yours too. You will realize that you get time for yourself if you really follow a stringent routine which helps you to become self-disciplined. The disadvantage of having such a manager is that you become the needle of a clock, always ticking and always running to complete things within the stipulated time. If by nature you are not like this, you will feel stressed about meeting deadlines.

The best way to handle such a boss is to flow with him. If you need more time, don't be afraid to ask for it. But make sure that you ask for it early rather than near your deadline. Another important aspect is to ensure that you never go unprepared to a meeting. He will come prepared with his own answers, and a lack of preparation on your part might force you to agree with his decision, which you could repent later. Have frequent communication with him so that he is not surprised towards the end because such type of a manager keeps calibrating his timeline based on the signals he receives from his team members. The biggest advantage with such a manager is that if he enjoys his work-life balance, he will let you enjoy yours too provided you stick to the timelines and schedules.

> *We don't get to cherry-pick our managers; but we can definitely learn to deal with them. Understanding distinct managerial styles and adapting to them is the Mantra to Success. Those who master the talent to tune in to different managerial styles, get plenty of leeway to devise their own means and ways at work. This isn't an innate talent—it can be learned and developed.*
>
> ~SANDEEP KOHLI, NATIONAL DIRECTOR-HUMAN RESOURCES, ERNST & YOUNG

16. MANAGER-CUM-OWNER

Congratulations, if you have risen to work directly with the founder/owner of a company! This doesn't mean that you've hit the glass ceiling and don't need any career tips. There are many examples where founders step aside to give way to more capable professionals to lead and take their companies to a new level.

There are broadly three types of such organizations: A professionally-run institution, a personality-driven organization and a family-run business. All three require different sets of career tips to ensure that your reporting to such a level is successful.

In professionally-run institutions decisions are taken based on merit and the founders give space and respect to people who bring specific skills to the table. They facilitate and ensure that the execution is aligned with the vision of the executive team. Sometimes founders may not agree with you or hesitate to try or let you try new things. You will need to remember that since the founders have a larger stake in the company, they could overrule some decisions. But it is done not based on position but on merit.

In a personality-driven organization, the only difference is that all major decisions need to have a complete nod from the head. Even though you may prepare an extensive presentation with bottom-up views and all the pros and cons, the final decision will always be from the top.

In a family-run business, the senior-most positions are usually reserved for family members, but even these are making a shift for professionals to lead them in this globalized and connected world. Also, sometimes the heirs may not be interested in pursuing the same business and move on. This paves the way for professionals to get prominent positions.

What Can You Do?

In a professionally-run institution, founders don't show off their founder tag but work like managers/peers with their management team. Even if they recommend a candidate, he still has to go through an interview panel. You will face less peer competition under such founders and they will ensure that everyone is tied with the single vision to make the company successful rather than focusing only on their own areas and covering their own backs. You need to work closely with your peers and the founders and work for the success of the company. This will provide you with a great chance for learning.

A word of caution: some founders are somewhat eccentric about taking the company to new heights and for this they will demand the world from you. You will have to cope with their whims and fancies. The best way to handle this is to recognize such traits. If you have a good idea or are passionate about something, present it with good justifications by keeping the company in mind rather than showing how smart or capable you are.

In a personality-driven organization, you could feel hurt that all your hard work is not appreciated by the owner. But you will also have mental peace because he will own up to his decision and you will be judged mostly on your execution. It might hinder your own decision-making skills and learning about how your decision could have been implemented, but don't let that bother you. Know that everyone who is reporting to him is capable and trustworthy else they would not be in the positions they are in. You may not need to put in an extra effort to win him over but you need to be prepared very well when you approach him because such owners sometimes become eccentric about doing things in a certain way. He could cross-check one's suggestion with another to make sure that he has all perspectives to make his own decision.

In a family-run business, loyalty matters the most. So if you are loyal and well-tuned to the ideology of the family and their way of doing things, you will be well taken care of. They need new skills, ideas and suggestions, so try to provide them with these and also look for more people who can help to take the business to new heights. Obviously it will take time for new hires to be trusted. Always keep refining your skills to make yourself relevant. You should be ready for any young heirs taking over and keep yourself updated with the latest trends and happenings to match with that of the younger people. So keep posted on new things in your field and update your skills or be ready to face a job loss or being sidelined when the generation changes.

In all these cases, you need to be extra careful in financial matters if you have the signing authority. Be sure before signing anything. If you feel pressured, give up the role of signing authority. Also, in the case of any discrepancies, know that the court will recognize you as the person who signs, and not the founder in case of any litigation. So always be aligned with the founders/owners. In case of a major disagreement where your values are compromised and your self-respect is at stake, quitting is the only option.

We live in a knowledge economy where highly capable people work towards a large vision, as a founder manager you can just enable and empower them.

~AMIT GUPTA, CO-FOUNDER, INMOBI

17. MANAGER'S FRIENDS, ENEMIES AND FRENEMIES

Have you ever noticed that a statement you just made about your project to someone outside your team has irritated your manager? You may not have said anything negative but just expressed your opinion on something. You will also be surprised that your casual joke to a colleague is used in your performance appraisal. Facing such flak, you stop talking to many people because you don't know who's spying on you and how it will affect you.

However, rather than going into a cocoon or blaming your work environment, try and understand why you are landing into such situations. Is it happening to others too? If yes, how have they handled it? If not, then why you? Is your manager known to do such things? Are other teams also facing a similar issue? Is the work environment such that friends and relatives of the management are hired in large numbers?

What Can You Do?

You need to be aware of your surroundings. As you grow in the organization, your interactions will start increasing and you will be more prone to such issues, especially if you don't know your manager's relationships with other people—be it your peers, his manager, his peers, and so on. Sometimes, managers share their frustration with some trusted employees.

Keep an eye on who he talks to—you will get some clues on his relationships. You could also keep an eye on the email content where you are copied and see the style of responses, etc., to know this. Gauge your interactions with those who might not be on the same side as your manager, but do not stop talking to such people. Just be careful about what you divulge to them. It should not be something that can backfire on you. These people are good in providing you with another perspective.

You might have made a mistake. There is no harm in owning up to it or accepting it. If you feel someone has twisted something out of context and fed it to him then do provide the exact conversation which took place. After a few mistakes, you will understand the undercurrents in the team and the others with whom your team interacts. Calibrate your discussions accordingly. Most times, it is not the actual project that causes the problem, it is something around the project, i.e., approach, root cause, dependency, misinformation, late information, wrong decisions and most importantly the blame game. So beware of commenting on such issues and if doing so back it up with your own proof and assessment.

> *Stakeholder management is the strongest catalyst in one's professional growth as a leader.*
>
> ~PINKESH SHAH, FOUNDER AND CEO, INSTITUTE OF PRODUCT LEADERSHIP

18. SAYING NO TO YOUR MANAGER

Saying no to your manager is an art and it requires skills.

People spend a lot of time thinking about how to say no, they rehearse a lot on choosing the right word, framing the right sentence and preparing all the possible responses to a manager's question. Try not to become so tense that when the actual meeting takes place, you cannot say what you have practised for days. You lose control on the conversation. If you feel guilty about saying no then it will reflect on your face. Any good manager will try to play that feeling to his advantage and ultimately, you may end up saying yes instead of no.

It becomes even more difficult to say no when your manager is well respected and maintains a good relationship with his team. If he is dependent on you and has taken good care of you, then you will appear even weaker during such conversations.

What Can You Do?

You have made up your mind to say no. If you get some new points during your meeting with your manager, don't change your answer, buy time to think again. If he makes you a promise that warrants you changing your answer, try and extract a rough timeline about when the promise will be fulfilled. Most promises are verbal. Your decision to change the response depends on your manager's image—does he keep promises? You could ask for a meeting with your manager's boss about the promise so that you can be doubly sure that both levels of managers are in sync and the chances of fulfilling it become higher. However, there are many situations where you want to or need to say no. Let us look at a few such situations.

The company and the manager have done a lot for you, but you want to leave the company. How can you tell your manager? You feel indebted to him for going out of his way to help you during a difficult patch in your life or career, or you've got the project you wanted and your compensation is always well taken care of. You too have given your best and supported your manager in all possible ways. However, you feel that it is time for you to move on so that you can learn new skills which are needed for your future. You feel guilty about wanting to leave, but you fail to recognize that your manager will in all probability not think about you when he gets a better offer. This is a professional world and all help, support and reciprocity is done in the interest of the company or the team. There is nothing personal in it, even if there is something personal, then let it continue even after you change the job. So instead of worrying and feeling guilty, go and tell him that you need his support in leaving the company and that you will continue to be in touch with him and seek his mentoring wherever required. Don't get entangled with the past. The manager may feel bad, but it is up to you to maintain your humility and respect. Sooner or later, you will see that your wish will be granted, even though it could be after multiple rounds of discussions. This could also be true while changing the team.

Always be prepared for situations where the manager does not come to terms with the 'betrayal', and even if he releases you, the relationship is damaged forever. Don't feel hurt or guilty about this: time will heal the relationship. Otherwise, just know that you have finally recognized your manager for what he actually is.

Another example: Be aware of the power games played at the managerial level—it could be with his peers or with his manager. How can you say no if you feel that you are a pawn in these power games? Refer to the career tip on building your own brand. If you are upfront, put all the facts on the table and argue your case based on the data before providing a reasonable explanation. That way, if the manager is wrong, he will not choose you because he will not want to take the risk of getting his statement negated by you in front of others. However, if the manager feels okay, he will certainly choose you to explain to his peers or management as you are known to be upfront. In this case, always speak the truth about what you know and stick to it without giving any colour to the explanation. If you have been asked to hide something or respond selectively, then it is up to you to agree or to say no. You should say no if the request is unreasonable, or feel the facts to be incomplete and incorrect, or if it will impact your brand/position. But if you are convinced of your manager's stand, then go ahead and support it. You should not chicken out in such situations because it will speak negatively about your leadership qualities. Just be consistent in your response irrespective of who is asking it.

Then there are some day-to-day issues like saying no to helping a colleague complete his project when you have completed your task well ahead of time. Take your decision to say no in such a situation keeping the larger interest of the company or team in mind rather than whether or not you gel well with your colleague. Such opportunities will not only give you a chance to know your colleague better, but also help you to a positive change in your working relationship with your colleague and also earn you brownie points from your manager. But when you just cannot avoid saying no, then tell your manager clearly. Sometimes you need to say no when you have taken up some course of study or have a family commitment. Again, if you make it clear to your manager right at the beginning, he will appreciate it. When your manager asks you to change the dates of your much-awaited vacation plan again take your time to think through. It could be for something that cannot be avoided, so, you need to consider it seriously, and if you still have to say no, be ready with a very strong reason for refusing.

Stick to your ground about saying no when you feel that you have been asked to do something, sign somewhere or send an email where it could be unethical, false, or if you are not sure of the facts and do not have a true picture of why you are doing so. Be polite while saying that you are not comfortable about doing it. If forced, try to meet with your manager's boss and HR to clear your doubts.

> *A skilful no reflects and imparts power in negotiations.*
>
> ~DISHAN KAMADAR, PROFESSOR IN ORGANIZATION
> BEHAVIOUR, INDIAN SCHOOL OF BUSINESS

19. HATING YOUR MANAGER

When you join an organization, your supervisor tries his best to make you successful because he has hired you and therefore wants to justify his decision. However, with the passage of time, it could happen that his style of communication, management, decision-making approach, team environment, etc., may not be to your liking.

It may be so that you are in a team where your manager is supportive of you, and consults you more often than necessary. In turn you enjoy being the so-called power centre within the team. Suddenly if he quits and a new person takes over your power diminishes and your status becomes equal to other team members. Naturally, you will not like this situation and blame the new manager. It could also be that the new manager might not see a need to assign you a special tag. He could have chosen someone else for it too. He has nothing against you, but could feel that your skills are not worth considering you at a higher level. This could lead to dissatisfaction over time, and you start disliking your manager.

Another situation could be that your peer has become the manager you wanted to be. Knowing his shortcomings quite well, you did not have much respect for him as a peer and now find it difficult to accept him as your new manager. This leads to a lot of resentment and frustration because you know that he is not really capable.

Sometimes, even if everything is the same, your manager's style of working conflicts with some of your key beliefs, thereby making it difficult for you to stand him. It could be his temper, his unpleasant words, his hard-hitting jokes, his ambiguous stand on serious issues, the way he treats his team or anything else that makes you feel repulsive towards your manager.

The first reaction to every such situation is to run away from such a job. You can do it if you are at an early stage of your career, but as you grow, you are sometimes stuck in a situation in which you have to face such managers for a longer period due to narrower options of suitable jobs. Other factors that could stop you from changing your job are good compensation or challenging and interesting work. These types of factors make you try to tolerate such managers as long as you can and also because the manager may not have the same negative feeling towards you.

What Can You Do?

You know it is not an ideal world, so try to adjust accordingly. Observe what triggers responses from your manager that repulse you. Observe whether his behaviour is different for you or is he like this with everyone? If he behaves the same way with everyone, then you are probably being oversensitive or you still have to learn how to minimize such incidences that hurt you. If it is happening only to you, reflect on what you do or how you approach him to warrant such a response. You cannot change him, but a good reflection will certainly help you to understand the situation better and thereby handle it too. It is important for you to realize that if you respect him, or if you feel that he takes care of you, even a harsh comment will not hurt you because of the level of high trust you have with him. However, when the bond is weak, even a small spark can cause heartburn.

One of the commonest complaints people have is about their manager micromanaging their work. Not only does he ask probing questions, he comes to your desk frequently to get the status. You can feel him breathing down your neck and passing comments, giving inputs or unsolicited feedback and soon, it becomes unbearable being around such a manager.

You need to accept that some managers are like this. They could be new to the role and therefore nervous about missing something. For some, it is more of a case of not wanting to look bad in front of his management in case something goes wrong with the project. Some may feel that you will miss the deadline and therefore keep asking about it. Here again, if you have a good relationship, you might not feel that bad. If your relationship is not so good, you will feel extremely untrustworthy or unskilful. You can overcome this with some effort by taking the initiative of providing your manager with frequent updates. Before he can even reach your desk, approach him with a smile and start giving him an update. Most of the time, this will reassure him and he will slowly reduce his micromanaging, but it never stops completely.

Most people tend to attribute their failures and frustrations to their managers. If you feel so hurt, you should try to tell your manager at least once. Say it in a way that is not so obvious—something like 'I know this is your style, but I feel like this'. What could happen? Either he will be sympathetic and change his style a bit or he could laugh and ignore it, or he could get very angry and upset with you. However, it is a risk worth taking. If you present the case well, the chances of the last option are bleak. It is also possible that he has already received such feedback and is aware of it. This will make your job easier—he will listen to you. You will have the satisfaction of letting him know, but remember—it is easier for you to adjust with your manager rather than expecting him to adjust to you.

In trying to change, think about what it is that you don't like about your manager. Is it the way he works? Is it the way he behaves? Although you owe it to your manager to provide honest feedback, this may be difficult to do directly for many. Try to find a specific example of what your manager does that irritates you, and play this back to him explaining that what he just did made you feel unsettled and why that happened. Also, think about what it is that you do that causes your manager to react in the way that upsets you. Think about the other senior people you interact with and think of why those relationships work well, then apply them to your manager. Try to imagine what it would be like if it worked perfectly, and set out a plan to achieve that vision.

Quitting a job is very easy but finding a fulfilling job is very challenging. So it is best to make a sincere effort to convert your current job into a fulfilling one before trying elsewhere. However, when things continue the way they are and you have tried everything possible, and there is still no improvement, then you need to look out for something else.

> *If you can't stand your manager, one of you has to change, or one of you has to leave—try the change option first.*
>
> ~PAUL WHITNEY, VP HUMAN RESOURCES, NIMBLE STORAGE

CHAPTER THREE

MANAGING YOUR TEAM

20. APPLE AMONG ORANGES

Are you an insecure manager reluctant to hire qualified people for fear of being eclipsed? You may be forced to hire such people as they come highly recommended or they perform very well during the interview. Sooner or later, word about their superior skills will spread and they will be in demand from various quarters. If you try to steal their credit or not extend it to them they may slowly become frustrated. They could resort to things like not keeping you in the loop or criticizing your suggestions or solutions in meetings, and having skip level meetings with better ideas and creative solutions to upstage you. If not managed properly, the friction between the two of you becomes very evident to others in the company and both of you could suffer. However, in this case, you will be more on the receiving end from your management if your subordinate's skills are valuable for the organization.

Some managers go even further and start changing assignments to clip their subordinate's wings. They could also use their favourite employees to play one against the other. If you fall in this category then you must realize that such moves usually fail because not having the best inputs is doing a disservice to your team and the company. You can appear to be winning in the short term, but will suffer in the long term. Team members who are watching your every move could sense the politics or injustice (because their sympathy is always with the employee) and slowly some of them, especially high performers, would try and transfer themselves out of your team.

Managers can make employees' lives difficult by other means too. By not giving plausible answers to explain the denial of a promotion; a below-par hike; not providing meaty assignments; and most importantly, by not keeping promises.

Conversely, there are employees who are difficult by nature. There are some who are very vocal—they are like loose cannons. They will not toe the party line, and spill the beans without knowing or even caring about manager's stand on the topic. Such people can speak on anything with passion and knowledge and forget their manager's perspective on the issue. Peers tend to enjoy such employees' company only if they are not the target, but in general they try to avoid teaming up with them or sharing new ideas. In this case, the manager will not be insecure because an employee who is vocal and rubs people the wrong way and not only him, is no threat to him. Some managers use such people for their own advantage. By convincing such employees that his viewpoint is contrary to his manager's peers or manager's boss, the manager will appear innocent and all the dirty work will be done by the employee. Some managers try to gain sympathy from their management on managing such difficult cases to extract brownie points.

Then there are employees who are rumour-mongers and incite people against new guidelines or policies. Such employees could also be bad mouthing someone or creating friction in the team.

What Can You Do?

How long can you be living in denial that your employee is better than you in some ways? Once you realize this fact, try to learn from him as being a manager it is impossible for you to be a master in all areas. Give him credit for what he has done and help him grow within your team first. If he is getting blocked or does not get enough opportunity in the existing role, facilitate his movement outside your team. Such gestures will increase your respect in the eyes of employees and the team at large, and improve your own standing in the management team.

Having such a person in the team and keeping him motivated is a challenge but if you do it well, the employee can take ownership of a specific activity freeing you to focus on other areas in the project. Such employees can take up more challenges too. So you will be able to take on more responsibilities and in this way, grow too.

If you want to compete with your team members, then compete in learning new skills. If you become competitive in trying to showcase that you can resolve problems in better ways, you are not helping your case. By 'showing them down' you are lowering your own role and in time the team members will sense your ulterior motives, unless you are collaborative in finding a better solution. This will take a hit on your brand as other team members will also see through your actions.

If you feel that an employee is arm twisting you or taking extra mileage due to his unique standing don't overreact, but once in a while you need to speak plainly to make it clear who the manager is. If his habit, approach or practice violates a norm, then provide the right feedback and if required, escalate it. If you are truthful, the person will realize his mistake and be careful in future.

Similar is the case of dealing with people who are vocal. Being vocal is not a problem if the person is just concerned about his area of assignment. However, in a team setting, they could rub against their peers and or the manager. In that case, a plain speak with facts is the first step to handling the situation. Organize a training session with the HR for them. If the person is well respected or the meeting is going to be controversial in nature, it is important to be in sync with such people beforehand to avoid damage. Such people cannot be ignored or boxed especially if they are high performers, but should be dealt with tact.

Employees who are socially active and are always on top of all office news and gossip can sometimes become mischievous especially when it is not easy to put the blame on them. Take up such issues head on only if you have enough evidence. But don't start the discussion by making him feel guilty. 'Listen to his side of the story and if necessary tell him in a subtle way to be more careful in future.'

If the employee has frequent outbursts and such situations

continue for some time, it is high time that you should come out clean first. Many a time it is the mismanagement of a situation or procrastination from your side that has a bad effect. Most of the time such outbursts happen when the employee has set some expectations based on discussions with you which is not happening on the ground.

> *It is always advisable to seek help from peers/ executive sponsors to manage the team member, who needs all round grooming. Special attention to these team members showing them your support and understanding, yet drawing a clear line of authority will go a long way in building a well-rounded team.*
>
> ~SHOAIB AHMED, PRESIDENT,
> TALLY SOLUTIONS PVT. LTD.

21. PERFORM OR...

You may face the challenge of not being able to get the best out of a person. Every employee cannot exceed expectations every time. However, what hurts them is that when they don't get even the expected output of work assigned. This puts additional burden on the other team members to meet the team goal by taking on more from those who are under performing. Since headcount is fixed, you face the dilemma of what to do with those who do not meet your expectations.

You may approach the problem in several ways: You may want to go soft on low performers because you have hired them, and if you act tough it would tell the management that you made a wrong decision. You may want to give the person another chance to succeed because removing him from the team or the company, will give out a wrong signal to the existing team members and create a fear psychosis. You may be worried that your image will take a hit if you act decisively and will discourage people from joining your team in the future. Again, you may just be tempted to use this as an excuse to give a lower rating to satisfy the lower portion of the bell curve as mandated by the HR.

Sometimes you may become so dependent on a few team members that you divide the task in such a way that they will do the critical parts. The mundane, boring, non-glamorous work is assigned to the ones you consider average to low performers. It is a chicken and egg situation because some employees get demotivated with such secondary work and therefore do a slipshod job. On the other hand, this could lead you to judge a person's performance based on the assigned job and not give him any other challenging assignments because he feels that he will not be able to do it well. You must realize that by limiting his growth you are not utilizing your team's full potential.

Like every manager you too must aspire to have a high-performing team, but you must realize that there will be low performers over time in the team. This could happen when the team is expanded and the bar for the new hires is brought down, or it could be complacency on the part of the existing team members. It could also be that the perceived work has become too mundane. Sensing the ground reality, you may start to set lower expectations, rather than take steps to uplift the team's performance. It is not always true that the employee is at fault for not giving his best. You must take the onus in ensuring that he does everything possible to perform better. You have to act firmly rather than dodge the issue. A lack of firmness in action on low performers will slowly start impacting the rest of the team. This could cause a doubt in your capabilities and slowly the team will start becoming dysfunctional.

What Can You Do?

If you are the type who does not want to take tough action against low performance, then you will have to bite the bullet in the future. If you are not at fault and employee's performance issue is well known in the team, then don't be afraid of taking a tough decision. You will be pleasantly surprised as the other team members will welcome such a decision. However, before taking any firm action, be sure that you have tried your best in trying to turn around the employee. Reach out to the HR, his peers and others who can help the employee through coaching or mentoring.

Identifying a low performer is a tough job. Low performance can be broadly classified into three categories and needs to be handled differently:

Skill Versus Job Mismatch: A person lands a new job hoping that he will fit in well or that he will learn a new skill, but he is not able to make it. In such a situation, you as the manager have to provide necessary training, assign a mentor and give him enough time to learn and perform. During this period, you should try to provide a conducive environment. Sometimes an employee thinks that he has got this opportunity because of his superior skills and lives in a false notion that he will do well. But when reality strikes, he is scrambling to save the project from running out of hand. Taking corrective steps soon will help to improve the situation tremendously. Then there are those employees who live in their past glory and therefore, live in a comfort zone. They fail to realize that all organizations are dynamic in nature and changes are always happening, and soon find themselves losing out to peers and falling in performance ratings because they don't upgrade their skills to suit the job requirement.

Whatever be the reason, never declare a person a low performer quickly. Be convinced that you as the manager have done everything possible to help him out, and that the person is also willing to learn and perform. In certain circumstances it takes months and in some others even a year or two for a full turnaround. If things do not improve, have a dialogue with him and try to explore what can be done to match his interests, skills and job.

Personal Or Professional Events Hindering Performance: There are multiple instances in which a bad phase in a person's personal life has an impact on his performance at work. Certain events like divorce, death in the family, a bad medical condition, a sour relationship, etc., have deep impact on work. In most such cases he may come out for help because the problems are so personal in nature. However, by just mentioning about a difficult personal situation while keeping the details at bay, an employee can ask for various flexibilities for a period of time. In such cases be supportive and put him on projects that are not so high pressure, or distribute some of his responsibilities to others for some time. He may need to work with his management and the HR to provide such options to the employee such as a leave of absence to take care of his personal challenges or grant him permission to work part time. Here, the onus is on the employee to apprise his manager and work with him to find a solution.

Not Being Managed Properly: It is your responsibility as the manager to manage your employee properly. You should provide him proper guidance and opportunity and also give periodic feedback for improvement. Sometimes, by working under a different manager, he may start performing. This could be attributed to the work environment, chemistry mismatch, or management style that hindered his performance. If this happens you should assess his skills objectively and instead of being vindictive or blaming him.

Try to understand the reasons for the dip in the employee's performance. Explore all other avenues to improve his performance. Some employees take years to excel in a new company, whereas managers have patience for only for a few months. Certainly you cannot wait that long, but you can put the person on the right path by trying to match his skill set with his job function, and also through mentoring and coaching.

If you are sure that you have explored all possible ways and failed, you can put the person on a performance improvement plan in which you can assign goals and track the progress, and at the end of the stipulated watch period, decide whether the person can continue or needs to leave. While this type of plan helps some employees improve, there are others who may need to take the tough call and quit. There may be some employees who choose not to participate in the performance improvement plan, and quit on their own.

> *This tip hits the nail on the head with the pragmatic approach to performance handling which is absolutely essential to building a successful organization.*
>
> ~PADMA REDDY, COO R&D, HEAD, SOFTWARE AG
> INDIA DEVELOPMENT CENTER

22. WHAT EMPLOYEES WANT

As a manager your life could be tough. You may spend long hours to cope up with your work load and still feel miserable for not being able to manage your team(s) well. You may sometimes find it difficult to identify what you should do to be more effective. If your subordinates are not open or free with you it will be difficult to identify the areas they need to improve. This growing distance between you and your employees will hurt the execution of projects. Of course, all projects have their ups and downs and will never run smoothly, but a well-bonded team is much better equipped to handle difficult situations. So what can you as a manager do to make a well-bonded team? You need to look into what your employees expect from you and take steps to do so.

What Can You Do?

Employees have many expectations from their manager while working on a project. A few are listed below:

Well-defined Goal And a Working Process: As a manager you need to put forth a well-defined and clear goal. Most of the time, the path to achieve it is not clear and you need to brainstorm with your team to find that path. As a manager, lead the discussion and step in when needed. Accept all ideas and reason them out instead of shooting them down or criticizing them immediately. Build upon these ideas so that the final outcome is a good mix that the team will feel proud of. Cross pollination of ideas across teams is even better. Finally, put together all the points to reach the common goal. Review your points at every milestone and take corrective actions, if required. Lead from front and provide all necessary support to the team to achieve the goal. Everyone in the team should get an opportunity to voice their opinions at meetings so that the best points can be incorporated. Final responsibility for all the decisions taken lies with you the manager.

The definition of process is the key to success. The process should not hinder the speed of execution. It should be a guideline with the relevant checks and balances that can help the project to stay on course. You like most managers may think that a bunch of high performers will deliver the result, but in the end you could be in for a shock. The project fails and team members are bad mouthing each other and the morale of the team is at its lowest. This happens mainly because the work process was not being followed, or if followed, there weren't enough checks and balances in the system to ensure its proper execution. Sometimes a project fails when there is a faulty work distribution among team members. Please distribute work based on an individual's forte and discuss this openly in the team meeting to get everyone's approval. It is important to pay special attention to these aspects in the beginning itself.

An Involved And Transparent Manager: As a manager you need to call for frequent short meetings with all your team members for a periodic status update. These discussions help to identify and handle the risks. During the execution cycle of a project, teams go through a roller coaster ride, and here your communication skills play a major role in steering the team. During this entire period they look up to you. If you are detached, the morale of the team goes down very fast. It is equally important for you to share all news—whether good or bad, if it is going to impact the project and quickly act upon them. Don't keep things to yourself—to either feel important or because you feel that it may not be important enough to be shared or to avoid unnecessarily alarming your team. In dilemma, err on the side of over communication. This is always better because it will make the team know that you are one of them.

A Trusting Manager Who Delegates Well: If you do not trust your team, you should not be managing it. Most of the time, employees don't have a say in choosing their managers and could land up having one who might not trust them. There is a distinction between trust and blind faith. As a manager you cannot have blind faith in anyone. You should ask the right questions, assess risks, provide timely support to avoid any unpleasant surprises. Trust will help you bond with your team members as they feel their capability is acknowledged and appreciated, their opinions matter, and they are involved in team decisions and activities. Trust takes time to build. A team can do wonders if it is trusted. This in turn leads to empowerment.

If a person is hired for a particular job, respect his suggestions and ideas related to his area of work and any case of disagreement should be dealt amicably. He should not feel that he has been countered frequently due to power play. The more you empower your employees, the more they take their job seriously and deliver with full accountability and responsibility. For some managers delegation is very painful and their teams just end up being pairs of hands and legs that dance to their tunes. Without proper delegation, even an intelligent team can become a puppet and competent team members will be looking for the first opportunity to jump the ship.

Proper And Timely Feedback: Don't hesitate to provide feedback thinking it could demoralize the employee and therefore productivity. This approach is fundamentally wrong. Timely feedback is always appreciated. You too should be able to take feedback from employees to be a connected team. The litmus test for a good team will be when team members resolve issues among themselves without escalating it to the manger.

Recognition Of Achievements And Celebration Of Milestones: It is important to celebrate the achievement of all milestones. It could be as simple as having an ice cream party or going out for a social evening. Major achievements could entail a cocktail dinner. Recognizing achievements are equally important. Some achievements are announced at town hall meetings or are given private recognition with awards or spot bonuses. Some organizations have a special peer recognition award, where employees can recognize each other. It is a myth that all recognition has to be a reward—just a few words of genuine praise can increase an employee's motivation.

If you imbibe these five traits, it will help you to bridge the gap between your employees and you, which in turn will make your team stronger and more effective.

> *The amount of time you invest in building trust, transparency and open culture within your team is directly proportional to the results team delivers.*
>
> ~RAMESH PHATAK, VICE PRESIDENT, INDIA R&D, SCHNEIDER ELECTRIC INDIA PRIVATE LIMITED

23. GAUGING THE PULSE

Don't just be a taskmaster and focus only on the task. If you operate like this then by not getting to know your employees well will be your blind spot. You may want to keep a distance with your employees so that you can maintain a no-nonsense environment. There are a few managers who also do not have good communication skills and cover up their weakness by avoiding unnecessary communication with employees.

If you maintain distance from your employees then you will be prone to nasty surprises. A simmering conflict between two employees under you might explode in a meeting in which your boss and/or other seniors are present. This could reflect badly on your management skills. By being aloof you can neither sense an upcoming attrition nor your team's dissatisfaction. Since you do not know why the work is suffering, the corrective steps taken by you could aggravate the situation. Some teams may have developed so many silos that the team productivity is taking a hit. The manager is unable to pinpoint the source of the problem because he does not have any idea of the pulse of his team. Some managers might want to feel safe in their positions and let team members fight their own battles. If you follow such a method of divide and rule then it will not help because you need your team members to work together to achieve the project goals. Sooner or later you either have to act or someone else will step in to clean up the mess and take over.

Some managers are more subject matter experts and do not have adequate people management skills to sense and deal with the issues. Such managers need help from the HR or their management to step in to handle people issues.

The work environment is forever buzzing with news. You as the manager need to be aware of the grapevine and alert about the issues brewing and can take preventive steps before it boomerangs or becomes unmanageable.

What Can You Do?

An office environment is incomplete without people chit-chatting on office issues. They form strong opinions, and might create rumours and misunderstandings, which determine the work environment. If a team, group or company is doing very well, most things are under control, but the first sign of bad news gets this circle buzzing. A good handling of opinion makers and their circles is an important function of a leader. Ignoring them is simply your ignorance.

Engage in periodic dialogues with your subordinates even when there are no issues. If you are not proactive and wait for your team members to approach you, it will be too late to react and your options will become limited. It is better to gauge their predicament and try to nip these issues in the bud. If you have developed an emotional attachment with your employees where they feel safe to confide in you, they will be a good source of information of what is happening within and outside the company. This is also an important way of quelling any contentious issues.

If you get a sense of something brewing between two or more subordinates you can act in multiple ways—facilitate an open feedback between the two so that each one will know what the other thinks. If the issue is in the work distribution or work overlap then this could be resolved by bringing clarity in the deliverables. Sometimes the issue could be due to some misunderstanding caused by hearsay, and that could also be resolved through an open discussion. The difficulty arises when there is already a lot of bad blood between the two. In this case it is better to keep their work as independent of each other as possible so that their interactions are restricted. If you are a manager of managers and there is bad chemistry between two managers, handle it within closed doors to avoid any disagreements or mistrust spilling into the teams and impacting the environment.

Sometimes a mischievous employee can create a misunderstanding between a manager and other team members. If you do not have a good pulse, you might fall into the trap. Some conflicts are good provided they are restricted to the project and not on the people because healthy, occasionally heated and passionate discussions might bring out better alternatives. However managing such discussions and steering meetings in such a way that it does not leave scars on anyone requires high level of management skills.

> *The subtle but very precise capture of what transpires today in organizations is a key ingredient where one observes breakdown in communications in teams resulting in discordant teams. The situation capture and the simple but easy-to-follow language makes this a great read and one that will evoke one to retrospect on one's own behaviour. Let us start taking those small steps that make great organization cultures based on trust and led by leaders who spread an aura of magnificence through their learned and many years of acquired wisdoms.*
>
> ~REJI THOMAS CHERIAN, SENIOR VICE PRESIDENT, CAPGEMINI INDIA

24. EMPLOYEE IS THE KING

After working for a good number of years when you are promoted to a managerial role your happiness knows no bounds. Your professional and social networking sites will reflect your new position quickly and your new business card will be used frequently—not for new business connections but to announce in social and professional circles that you have arrived. This euphoria dies down fast when responsibility increases. The helplessness in getting work done by someone and still being responsible for the deliverables is a tough job. It is a test of how you treat your employees and how well you work with them. The nervousness of meeting deadlines and the frustration of not getting things done in a right way within the stipulated timeline forces you to goof up. You tend to force your own way hardly waiting to see the merit of another approach in your hurry. As they will not be able to finish the task within the timeline you expected, you will start questioning the speed of execution. If such incidences repeat, it will become evident to your team that you don't consider them dependable.

It is always a challenge to get something done by others in the way you would have done it. This tendency makes you micromanage your team or ask your co-workers frequent questions. This will be perceived as doubting their capabilities or finding fault in their work. It is very important to provide the right checks and balances, however in practice, if not used appropriately or without any empathy, it shows up as a lack of trust. To find their way out of such frustration, some employees use it to their advantage and dump their own work on managers like these. Just to show that you have superior skills and knowledge, you take their monkey on your back and soon find yourself sitting in someone's chair looking at his laptop, while he sits beside you. You get immense pleasure in doing the work the way you wanted it done in the first place but fail to realize that you are being taken for a ride by your team! Soon you will find yourself overloaded and focused only on a few activities and thus missing out on other more important things that could impact your own performance. Your colleagues could start looking for a change for lack of new learning or unwanted interference, causing you to lose good workers. All this because you have not transformed into a managerial role. It takes years to realize that you have grown because you have people to lead and they are willing to be led. You are more dependent on them than they are on you. Remember, your team can be led by any other manager who could be better than you.

What Can You Do?

As you grow in role and responsibility, you need to develop humility. Treat everyone with respect. It is not unheard of to find a manager reporting to someone in his team in the same company in the future. It could also be that some team members who have quit and started their own company approach you to help them to scale their business operations. There is nothing wrong in reporting to someone who once reported to you. When a person's career spans over decades, anything is possible and it is important to understand this.

Do you really think that you need to be better and more knowledgeable than each of your employee? Isn't this a tall order and an impossible goal? Such thinking will restrict your team's performance and will do nothing for your individual performance. You could be good in one area, and your team members in others. Leverage such complimentary skills for superior results. It is never expected for a manager to know everything. You don't have to show off your skills to prove you are better than others, but your position demands that you facilitate getting the work done. Helping your team when they need it, trusting and guiding them when they desire it the most will bring a positive environment that will give huge dividends. Certainly your experience will help them, but if you put yourself before your team, over time you will suffer. As a first time manager you will need some time to adjust to the new responsibility, and the earlier you realize it, the better it is for you.

You must know that you cannot take your employees for granted. If a few of them complain against you, the management will listen to them. You might be able to deflect it once but beware that such complaints can plant doubts in the minds of the senior management. If it repeats, then you are in for trouble. At the first whiff of such complaint, you may turn vindictive and start weeding out such employees but there is no guarantee that a new set of employees will not complain against you. So be cognizant that your job and growth are dependent on employees who support you.

If you nurture the feeling that you need to serve your team members, you will see a renewed energy in the team with greater bonding and better results. This will greatly elevate your standing in the organization.

> *Consider yourself as a resource available to your team to help them succeed in their goals; your goals will automatically be achieved.*
>
> ~PARI NATARAJAN, CEO, ZINNOV

25. PLAYING FAIR

As a manager it is natural to aspire to become popular among colleagues, and go overboard in pleasing them. This will make you popular within your team, but cause heartburn to others. If it happens once through oversight, it is fine; however, when it happens frequently it leads to huge ramifications in the wider organization, such unilateral actions are normally looked down upon. Some managers take it in their stride and improve, while others just swing to another extreme and slowly the team will start seeing changes in him and his popularity will wane.

Being a popular manager and being a successful one are

two different things. Often popular managers are successful too, but not always. One of the major ingredients to becoming a successful manager is to bond with people. Such managers know their team members very well. They pepper their conversations with personal touches without intruding on their privacy which makes their colleagues trust them. The crux of all manager–subordinate relationships is trust, and not issues about salary, designation, awards, etc. When they know that there is nothing to worry about because their manager will take care of any issue that arises, they will work better.

This could also be a sign of being a popular manager, but a popular manager will not take tough decisions so as not to antagonize people. A successful manager could still remain popular, but has to act in the wider interest of the organizational goals. If there is honesty in giving explanations, clarity in actions and finding solutions to difficult problems, the manager will be respected. Even if a few employees may get agitated with his decisions, he will earn their respect in the long term.

People are smart and they will find out whether the manager is just a taskmaster or a taskmaster with a heart. There is always an expectation to deliver more in a short span of time. People can do it once or a couple of times, and a good people manager can make the environment less stressful and involve himself at critical times to ensure that his team can deliver consistently with the least amount of stress.

What Can You Do?

As a manager earn your respect rather than demand it. Respect is directly proportional to a person's behaviour rather than his position. The most important lesson to be learnt is that you need to be fair in applying company polices, practices, rules and regulations without bias or favouritism. A person's growth can be tied with his performance, but tweaking a travel policy for someone you like and being strict with another whose performance is just average, will not speak of fairness. Being flexible in leave policy and being extra generous in allowing a high performer or a favourite person to work from home while being rigid for others is another reason for heartburn. Be fair and avoid this kind of favouritism.

Another type of issue that comes up is when a manager practices favourtism. Such double standards can put off employees completely. This becomes more acute when the team is very diverse, e.g., age, ethnicity, language, and so on. Hence, being consistent, courteous and respectful in your dealings and a good listener are the traits you need to develop for a sound team.

All managers have their favourites—they could be go-getters, problem solvers, good networkers who can get the right resources quickly, and so on. Never feel guilty about having favourites, but if you cross the thin line, where a few people benefit more than others unduly, then that becomes a problem. These benefits could be in project allocation, promotions, compensation, customer accounts, budget allocation and others. It is important to ask yourself three questions:

1. Do my team members see that I care for them?
2. Am I able to convey my decisions to them by looking into their eyes and speaking the truth? Organization truth always trumps over personal truth.

3.   Do I consider all the pros and cons before taking any action?

You are the best judge. If you feel that you have done the right thing and are able to explain your rationale, then you are done. Some people may not accept your reasoning, but they know why you have done it. You cannot do anything more than this. If you follow the above three values and walk the talk, over time you will earn the respect you deserve and develop an increased bonding with your team.

> *Successful leaders are sincere, honest and open-minded. They often listen most, willing to be challenged of their strongest convictions and yet remain humble.*
>
> ~RAJ RAGHAVAN, COUNTRY HR DIRECTOR, AMAZON INDIA

CHAPTER FOUR

MANAGING YOUR PEERS

26. PEER PRESSURE

Peer relationship is the most difficult relationship to manage at your workplace. The best joke in the workplace is normally at your manager's expense. It relieves tension and binds you with your peers. You may share a joke or laugh together, but when it comes to work the scene changes as you may choose to operate within your well-defined boundaries. If you are ambitious you would like to be ahead of your peers in climbing the corporate ladder. Your achievements might make them jealous. This is what turns the work environment murky. Peers see each other as threats in their career growth. A simple test would be to ask your peers to choose a leader in the absence of your manager. Most likely there will be no headway as they will not be able to arrive at any consensus due to conflicting self-interests.

You can never be in a position (other than being the head of an institution) of not having a peer in your office. They are the first set of people who will provide an opportunity to learn about interpersonal skills, balancing diverse ideas and taking criticism. It is important to learn to collaborate and win. It is difficult to ignore or avoid your peer if you don't like him because of the interdependence of work. Hence, it is better to focus on issues rather than on the person to overcome some of the interpersonal issues that can crop up in such interactions and make things worse.

Your relationship with your peer is dynamic. It changes due to many reasons: promotion, a new project or responsibility. You can save the relationship if you deal with it with maturity. Careers are long therefore, unpleasant incidences should just be taken as temporary setbacks.

Failure in handling peer relationships could lead to hurdles in your career growth.

What Can You Do?

There is no single mantra for positioning yourself among your peers. Having been in the company for a long time and worked in the same team for years, some people's feelings might have hardened against their peers. It could so happen that a new peer with a clean slate may go ahead of the old-timers who keep opening their old wounds and stay put in their careers. However, people do change and so do their equations with other people. Some changes are due to self-realization, while others are events outside their control that have forced them to change. For example, changes in organizational structure or changes in company direction, etc., can bring arch rivals together against a bigger common threat.

Be aware of your peers' projects, so that you can help them in time of need. Help out your peer to answer a difficult question if he is unable to or at least prompt him. If your peer has made blunders that have affected your project, the easy way out is to expose the blunders to earn brownie points with the management. The more difficult way is to make others aware of it by providing a positive solution that focusses on the issue and not on your peer. This shows maturity and will be appreciated by both your peers and the management.

Many a time you may avoid giving suggestions for fear of being rejected or laughed at, but if you have to maintain a lead over your peers, you need to be creative in giving suggestions. Don't restrict yourself to giving suggestions only in your area of work—present them as an overall benefit for the project. It is also important to understand that only those who show an initiative or are proactive in projects and organizational matters get an edge over their peers.

Risk-takers takers sense an opportunity and grab it when others are still thinking about its pros and cons. Such people rise faster than their peers who have caged themselves into their comfort zones. In such situations either you learn from your peer's growth and prepare to rise, or find solace in blaming office politics, your manager, peers, etc., for missing the opportunity. Be flexible, helpful, have a good knowledge in your area of work and push the envelope to shine above the rest.

> *Peer relationship management is key to a successful corporate career and the useful suggestions offered in this book are very practical and easy to adopt.*
>
> ~RAMKUMAR NARAYANAN, GM, EBAY PRODUCT DEVELOPMENT CENTRE, INDIA

27. DIFFICULT PEER

If you are lucky you will have peers who are cooperative and work together to make a project successful, which makes teamwork more interesting, enjoyable and fruitful. Not only does this provide a healthy environment of learning, but it creates a sense of achievement too when they outperform each other by setting higher goals. There are numerous examples when peers have gone beyond their call of duty in helping others to complete their assignments in the bigger interest of the project. This type of work environment is conducive for the growth of the company and the management plays a key role in building this environment of collaboration.

However, there could be some peers you just cannot stand as they either lack subject expertise or you feel that they are acting too high and mighty. Some could be interfering or bossy or some could be very generous with their unsolicited advice. It could also be that the peer has stolen credit which was due to you. The list goes on. As time passes, you will tend to avoid these types of colleagues as much as possible, which might adversely affect teamwork.

You cannot totally ignore your peer as your work is in some way tied with his, which might indirectly affect your own performance at work.

What Can You Do?

It is likely that your peer is also finding it difficult to team up with you. The choice for both of you is either to carry forward such animosity or come to some neutral ground for the sake of the project or the company and most importantly for your own mental peace. Your strained relationship is also a strain on your manager, who would not want warring team members. It is best to focus on the issue rather than the person. For example, if you had an unpleasant email exchange with your co-worker don't shut him out, continue to provide your perspective and involve a wider audience relevant to the subject being discussed so that they too can also provide their viewpoints. Of course, you must also evaluate your own style of communication, both verbal and written, which might be the cause of the problem.

Do you have the same types of issues with your other colleagues too? If yes, then most of the blame will come to you for poor teamwork even if you are right. Therefore, first try to mend fences in order to grow in your organization. It is okay to have divergent views on any topic with any number of people, but when the issue becomes personal, it is time to back off.

> *Very practical advice on dealing with difficult peers, which we can all benefit from by applying at our workplaces.*
>
> ~RAKESH AERATH, VICE PRESIDENT CONSULTING SERVICES, CGI INDIA

28. PEER POWER

If your peer is a high performer then it is ideal to team up with him. A great working relationship with such type of peers will certainly help you to take your career forward. You may think that if you are associated too closely with such people, you could appear to be second fiddle to them and that could be counterproductive to your ambition of growth. But this can only happen if your own standing in the team is weak and you have the reputation of being more of a follower than a leader. However, sometimes this could work another way—you could learn from them, and over a period of time you might be able to turn around your performance and improve your standing in the team.

If you are good in your work and reach out to such peers as and when you need help, you will be considered as a collaborative person. You could also team up with such peers for projects, and they can be of great help. If you are stuck in a situation and are clueless about which way to proceed, reach out for suggestions. Even if your manager comes to know about it, you will probably not be robbed of the credit because you are reaching out to a peer rather than asking your manager to intervene. If your work depends on a person or a team with whom you don't have much interaction, you may not get the attention you seek because they have their own priorities to work upon. However, if you have a good relationship with them, they will go out of their way to help you.

Don't hesitate to approach such a high-performing and well-connected team for help for fear of being turned down. Remember that the chances of refusal are less if the peer also sees value in a partnership with you. While reaching out, sometimes you need to be patient as people take time to respond. It is equally important for you to build a relationship because once it is in place, the probability of an affirmative response is higher.

Sometimes the hiccup in approaching such peers could also be because of a behavioural issue. He may be known for his attitude, ego or his repugnant style of communication. You need to be thick-skinned and tactful in dealing with such people. It might turn out that he is unlike his reputation. If you manage to team well with him it will give you an added bonus, as others could not succeed in this.

Some high performing peers can slowly develop a superiority complex as they know that they are in high demand. It is important for them to realize that if they don't check their highhanded attitude immediately, they could face resistance in moving up.

What Can You Do?

It is important to understand that as you grow in your career, and the competition among peers heats up, collaborative skills are appreciated and respected. But this does not mean that you are surviving because of their support. It simply means that you are someone who is putting the company before self. So it is better that you go for it even though it is difficult to tolerate an irritated peer. With the passage of time, such behaviour might not appear that irritating.

It is not always true that it is only you who needs help from such peers. You can also help them, as you know some of their weaknesses and can help them as well. Once your peer starts trusting you, he too can seek your help. Sometimes meetings become ugly if the high performer has a reputation of rubbing people the wrong way. In such cases, it is better to reach a common understanding before the meeting.

At times, such peers insult people not only in meetings but also otherwise. They know what they do and how they are perceived. As they mature in their role and experience, they may want to take steps to change themselves and this is where they could seek your help in repairing soured relationship with some of their peers.

It could also happen that your good relationship with such a peer can take a hit. He could start seeing you as a rival due to your unique skills, and might start showing his back on some issues. It is important that you don't change because he might be damaging himself and both your team and manager can see the change in him.

> *It is a reality in corporate life that more often than not, you do not get to choose your peers. Therefore, it is important to make the best of what you have got, especially because tasks in organizations are increasingly becoming collaborative in nature. If you have a high performing peer, surely she will have some qualities/competencies that are appreciated by the organization, which helps her to achieve organizational objectives. Therefore it is necessary to learn from her and seek complementarities with your own competencies. If you have a Ronaldo or a Messi in your team, you are better off providing an assist rather than trying to score yourself. Living with their tantrums and being overshadowed by their achievements are relatively small prices to pay for the organizational success. If you are confident about your abilities and how you are adding value to the organization, you should never be afraid of depending on others.*
>
> ~SOURAV MUKHERJI, ASSOCIATE PROFESSOR AND CHAIRPERSON P G (MBA) PROGRAMME, INDIAN INSTITUTE OF MANAGEMENT BANGALORE

29. WATCHING YOUR BACK

As you grow in the organization, you will be bound to find people who will try to sabotage or hijack your or others' achievements. This situation arises if a person sees another as a threat or an obstacle in his career.

Bitterness among peers arises due to failed projects in the past or unresolved misunderstandings. It could also be the result of unclear policies in the organization or a lack of consistent implementation of policies which can create an environment of mistrust.

People are more worried about complaints and criticism from peers with whom they don't really gel. Usually even if such cases are evident to the team, not much importance is given to them as your sour relationship with that peer is well known. However, what is most damaging is when people in your close circle start backbiting. These are not rare occurrences and can happen very subtly without you even realizing it.

The manager always knows the vibes between people in his team and if the person has a reputation of not being on good terms with you, then he will take all such complaints against him with a pinch of salt. But if he gets negative feedback from someone you are considered to be on good terms with, then your manager will certainly listen, and that is the real reason for you to be alarmed.

This backbiting could vary from trivial to more serious matters. It is not only restricted to when you are in a mess. Even if you have done a great job and are basking in the limelight, a person bent on sabotaging your good moment can email your manager casting aspersions on you. It depends how the manager handles such cases. He could ask for proof and handle it smoothly at his own end without you coming to know about it, or he could ask you directly for clarifications and if required, call for a three-party meeting. A manager could also choose not to do anything with such information till such time he needs to and you will be totally unaware of the opinion your manager is forming about you.

What Can You Do?

The default way to deal with peers with whom you mostly end up in a conflict is to avoid interaction with them until absolutely necessary. If you are a manager or work in a team where you can delegate work to avoid confrontation, then do it.

However, you must know that you cannot really escape your peer for long. One approach could be to have an open communication with him and understand why he feels the way he does about you. If he takes this opportunity and is upfront with you, then listen to him, thank him and then share your own concerns. Most of the time, it just requires an ice breaker to patch up things. If you feel that you were wrong in the past and it has impacted the relationship adversely, then you should apologize. This is one of the most powerful tools in resolving misunderstandings.

Another approach is to start communicating about non-controversial topics. It takes patience and perseverance to continue such interactions and when you see some positive momentum, you can slide in some thorny issues too. Sometimes mistrust runs so deep that only words may not be able to repair the damage. Result-oriented actions are required to slowly regain the trust. However, in some cases, in spite of your best efforts, there is no progress so you can either live with it or ask the HR or manager to provide you with an external facilitator who can help in building a communication channel with the peer.

If you have already had a few meetings which were inconclusive, then it is a good time to get your manager involved to help you resolve your differences. If you feel that the manager will always take the side of your peer, then you need to improve your own relationship with your manager first. Have open and frequent communication with him so that he starts understanding your point of view.

Now let us look at another scenario. What happens when you are known to be in the good books of your peer, and someone is doing something behind your back? If this is initiated by your manager, then it is better that you put all the facts on the table and focus on the issue. This will help you immensely. If you come to know through some other source, talk it out, but in a way that you understand what was said and in what context. Sometime the tone and content get twisted when the information reaches you and leads to misinterpretation. If your peer has done it on purpose to spite you, he will try to cover up. If you pose the question to him in a calm and composed manner, it will have a bigger impact on him. If he has not done it and someone has twisted the facts, he will thank you for checking it out with him. Either way you win.

> *Timely and proper communication works wonders to remove any misunderstanding.*
>
> ~PROF. S. SADAGOPAN, DIRECTOR, IIIT BANGALORE

30. PEER FEAR

Competition among peers is natural and it becomes stark when one among you is promoted. As organizations are becoming flatter, the wait to grow is also becoming longer. The problem of stagnation in career might be compounded further when the organization is not growing and the higher positions become scarce.

If you are an ambitious person, the first thing you will do is to look around in your peer group, to gauge your own chances of moving up. You may think that your colleagues with greater years of experiences would be promoted. Sometimes you may find most of your peers have more or less the same skills if not better ones and therefore wonder what will differentiate you over them. Sometimes you may think that some of them have been in the organization for a longer period, so they will be considered before you. Your doubt on whether you are getting blocked in your career will be further strengthened when your project is not giving you the right visibility. You find a lack of space where you can shine.

It is important to understand why someone becomes more visible than you. There are a few who are by nature good in selling their achievements, but they cannot do it unless they have a special skill or have a stronger grip on the area of their work, else such boasting or selling would fizzle out. If you are equally or nearly good, and if you feel your work will be recognized on its own, then you are wrong. You need to make it visible to others.

If you feel that you still have to learn more before you aspire to grow, then it is better to learn from your peers and others in the organization. Don't spend productive hours thinking of being in an imaginary race and feeling having lost to your colleagues rather than spending time to focus on the areas where you need to improve or to further build on your strengths. Because when an opportunity comes, it might not give you time to prove yourself, and someone else will be pip you to the race. It is equally important to increase your interactions with the stakeholders of the next level and to make them aware of your contributions, skills and your capabilities.

What Can You Do?

Is leaving the only option? It is certainly one of the options. You can leave the team and look for opportunity in other teams in your company. If seniority means that you will get more decision-making opportunity and more responsibility to act, then it is better you look for that. If seniority means a heavier designation, then be careful as it could be misleading. Sometimes a higher designation in another team or company might not always mean higher responsibility. Your motto should be to not only take on more responsibility but to learn well.

Here are the pitfalls of always wanting to be a senior in the team for career growth: You may be so busy in mentoring or helping juniors that you would be left with less time to learn new skills or areas. Initially this appears to be in line with what you wanted, but soon you will start losing out with your peers in the industry for not keeping pace with new skills and knowledge. Many a time learning from experienced peers and seniors is so important that it is good to have them in the team.

However learning and growth go hand in hand and therefore once you have learnt enough, you can seek other opportunities where you can apply such knowledge, if the way up is becoming difficult in the current position. But you should keep in mind that your new position should continue to provide new learning opportunities.

Patience also pays. Say for example, if most of your so-called senior co-workers are well-respected and capable, they might also be feeling stagnated and they might also look out to join other teams (as the company grows), or quit the company therefore paving way for you to rise. It could also be a newly hired peer who can come in competition with you, if he has superior skills. Sometimes you assume that a peer (senior in experience or tenure in the company) will be chosen over you, but it could happen that you get chosen. It also happens that multiple positions are opened and more than one person can get opportunity to rise.

So your decision to quit should be totally on your skills, experiences and timeline, and should not always be influenced by your positioning among peers, as this changes with time.

> *Competition drives excellence and follows you, wherever you go. Take the challenge and let it bring out your best.*
>
> ~SOUMITRA SANA, EX- HEAD OF NOKIA TECHNOLOGY CENTER, BENGALURU

31. PEERITISM

Favouritism is a common malady. You may think that bringing such an issue to the management's notice does not help as it could be a matter of perception.

Some employees complain about the murky work environment because of their manager's favouritism. Stories of helplessness to shine or to rise against a manager's favourite are not unheard of in the work place. At times there could be more than one favourite in the team.

You may either learn to live with it or contemplate changing the team or company in order to rise. But there is no guarantee that you will not face the same problem in the new organization too.

What Can You Do?

First try to understand what skills your manager's favourite person is bringing to the table. Is he a troubleshooter? Is he a good networker? Or is he simply a positive guy who will infuse positive energy even in the wake of a crisis?

Hone the qualities that can make you your manager's favourite. Your manager need not have only one favourite. The one who volunteers to bail out the manager from a mess is likely to become his favourite. Employees having more complementary skills than their managers or even simple skills like the art of conversation or thinking out of the box, can become their favourites Praising your manager to his boss on the skilful handling of any sensitive or critical issue could also go a long way to get you brownie points. But make sure it does not appear as an act of sycophancy.

But if you find that your manager is giving someone out-of-turn benefits in a secretive way or giving opportunities to someone he likes who may not necessarily be the best for the job, etc., then the best way to deal is to talk with your manager. This will help in removing misunderstandings if the act is unintentional, and if the manager has done something knowingly at least he will be more careful in future. You can also escalate to your manager's boss or even to the HR if the issue bothers you immensely. But try to take it up with your manager first before escalating it.

It is better to reflect on the problem rather than go by what people say. The situation has arisen due to a lack of trust between you and your manager, or because of inadequate communication. It could also be that you have not asked the right questions to get the right response. It could also be that you are so convinced about being victimized that no answer from your manager can ever convince you, however honest it is. It could also be that someone in your team keeps inciting you, thus not helping you to look beyond the issue. When you discuss it with your manager, do it with an open mind without prejudice and try to understand his point of view. You might not agree to it, but listening is important. If nothing helps then it is better to focus more on work and improve your skills rather than wasting time on something that is not under your control.

> *You should strive to be regarded as the best leader/ manager by your fair-minded peers, and this requires you to truly be a very good leader rather than being*

able to manage your manager well; if you can achieve this, you need not worry about favouritism by your manager.

~NARESH SHAH, PRESIDENT, EG INDIA R&D,
HEWLETT PACKARD

CHAPTER FIVE

MANAGING YOUR MANAGER'S BOSS

32. THE BIG BOSS

You must be aware of the importance of nurturing a relationship with the manager's boss. However you may be naïve in managing it. There could be various reasons for not putting in the effort towards building such relationships. You may put the onus on your manager to keep their bosses updated about your skills and achievements, or you may wait for the big boss to initiate interactions. You may feel hesitant to approach them because you don't know how to make the first move or you may not want to disturb him unnecessarily. It could also be that the manager's boss is perceived as being very reserved, hierarchical in nature or ill-tempered, so you dare not approach him, or you may feel that your manager will feel offended if he finds out that you are mingling with his boss.

Be smart and try to find opportunities to gain more visibility.

What Can You Do?

There are many ways to increase your visibility. Don't just focus on your assigned work, you must realize that visibility also comes by signing up for activities that are not directly assigned to you. So sign up for organization level initiatives or lead activities that are externally recognized and those that bring kudos to your team indirectly.

Some projects are high priority for your manager's boss. It is important to identify these and take a lead in such projects so that your interactions with him increase. Try to accompany your manager to meetings in which you can give part of the presentation from your manager's presentation deck.

Other avenues can also get you visibility. Sometimes corporate or division emails ask for suggestions to which most people don't respond. Those who do, earn some brownie points. Another way to become visible is to be proactive during a crisis. Representing the organization or a division in an external activity (for example, sports, quiz, theatre) can also provide the much needed visibility. Taking part in symposiums, presenting papers, applying for patents and getting customer appreciation are some other ways to gain visibility in the eyes of the big boss. Don't forget to thank him back when he congratulates or acknowledges you!

It is also important to win the trust and respect of your manager so that he can talk highly about you. This, along with your initiatives to interact with your manager's boss will certainly help you go a long way.

It is possible that due to certain personality traits of the manager's boss, it might take longer to break the ice. But don't despair because that is not in your control. You can only try to be focused and patient to get the slew of benefits that you want.

> *Out of sight is out of mind. In a large organization, serendipitous encounters must be purposefully engineered in order to get relevant facetime.*
>
> ~BHAVIN TURAKHIA, CEO, DIRECTI

33. THE FUTURE BOSS

Every organization has its own process for planning succession. This process ensures continuity in the business by making sure that key positions are filled up in case of any attrition. Some organizations cover only their middle or senior management under such plans while some others extend it to junior management levels. In fact, some companies do it for their critical senior non-management positions too. This planning exercise is normally done once a year and reviewed periodically.

The way organizations take up succession planning may be different, but the fundamental approach is the same. Against every position, there is a person identified to backfill the position. If the identified person is not ready in the short term, then some training is identified for him to be ready in the near future. It is not mandatory that the successor would be chosen from the team only. In some cases the successor could be picked from another team too. In certain cases, when the organization cannot identify a successor from within the company, they hire from outside.

Does the manager play a role in deciding his own successor? He can suggest or recommend someone if asked, but it is usually the responsibility of his boss to have the succession plan in place. It is also a norm for the manager's boss to discuss with his boss before deciding a successor for his employee. Usually a person is not informed that he is in succession plan for a particular position because not only does it raise unnecessary expectations in the person but there is also a likelihood that during the next review cycle, a new name could pop up as a successor. Sometimes there exists an obvious choice within the team, a second-in-command. However, no one can afford to take this position for granted, as with the passage of time, a smart hire could turn out to be a high performer, and join the race of succession.

If the manager exits, the logical choice is to kick in the succession plan. However, in certain circumstances, due to a change in the business scenario or something else, the kick-in doesn't happen, and two teams might be merged together or the existing team might be divided into a few sub teams. The company could also want to set a new charter for the team and would prefer a different skill set for the leader that could be hired only from outside.

What Can You Do?

You would certainly want your name to be among those discussed for your manager's succession. But how will you know if you are there? There are some easy signs to help you find out where you stand. For example, when your manager goes away on a vacation, who does he select to take his place? Some smart managers avoid giving any such indications for the natural successor and instead choose a few senior people as the signing authority. Other managers put multiple names in their out-of-office emails based on their areas of activity to avoid giving a specific name.

If you are in any of the lists, do not wither away such opportunities. The management may want to wait for the manager to return to take critical decisions, but there will be times when your manager's boss could approach you for something or you have to approach him for a crisis or decision. Going into minute day-to-day details will not only irritate him, but also cause him to miss the main point. Be specific when you narrate the problem to him—fit in all the details, but make it crisp. This will help him form a positive impression of you. Try and provide a few solutions to the problem too and seek his opinion. Even if he asks you to wait for the manager to return, you have an opportunity to interact with him and provide suggestions. So make most of the opportunity, but ensure that you understand his perspective and keep that in mind while doing discussions. All interactions go a long way whether positive or negative, so prepare yourself well. In situations where the big boss needs some data or information, act wisely and in the right way. Sometimes people tend to provide so much data that sifting through it for the exact answer becomes a challenge and therefore is not appreciated.

If your name is not in anyone's 'out of office' emails, then you are not being projected as someone solely responsible for a critical area. For this, you have to work harder. You may want to maintain the status quo as you believe that you do not have enough experience, or you have not been long enough in the company, or you are not part of the clique that has an excellent understanding with the management. All these could be true, but think about it—have you tried enough to make your own presence felt so that you could be considered as well? The organization is always dynamic and your work, network and soft skills will help in achieving it.

Once you feel that you are in the succession planning, you don't need to wait for your manager to quit, but make sure you continue to enhance your skills. Widen your network at office to become aware of career-advancing opportunities so that you can talk to the management whenever any position is available or likely to become available.

> *This is a great tip on how to progress well in one's career. Understanding your manager's top priority or pinpointing and proactively solving them by working together with the team will help your manager and manager's manager to view you as a potential successor. Remember, a promotion to the next level means you are perceived as already performing at that level. But while you do this, make sure you come across as solving first for the team's outcome and not for your career.*
>
> ~VIJAY ANAND, VICE PRESIDENT AND MANAGING DIRECTOR, INTUIT INDIA DEVELOPMENT CENTER

34. BOSS ALMIGHTY

You may look up to your manager for progression in your career. It is not wrong to do so—it is the manager's responsibility to look after employee aspirations, and he is the one who aligns a person's ambition with the organization's goal to achieve a win-win situation. Although most requests fall under the purview of the manager, there are some that are far and beyond what your manager can take a call on.

The person who can really help you out is your manager's boss. Through him, you can find opportunities in different groups that could be of interest to you. Sometimes your manager may have reservations in allowing you to be transferred as you may be working on a critical project or to avoid starting a trend. Your manager's boss may agree with him, but it is also possible that he will try to provide solutions to your manager's concerns without impacting your movement.

If your manager grows in the organization, there will be more opportunities for the growth of the people under him too. But at a certain point of time, due to the pyramid structure of the organization, your manager might stagnate. Your ambition to grow might take a beating and you may want to seek other opportunities to move up. For this, the best way to do so is to seek help from you manager's boss while keeping your manager in the loop. Your manager's boss has a stake in also deciding who will attend the prestigious training programmes that identify the so-called fast trackers. Your manager's boss could also suggest your name to other committees or fora which have a wider impact within the organization and therefore, give you an opportunity to network and widen your sphere of influence. He could also put your name down to represent the organization in external events, thus providing you visibility in the industry too.

What Can You Do?

Being in your manager's good books is the first step, but you also need to be in his boss's good books! Please ensure that you are well-respected, trusted and appreciated in the work that you do. But that alone cannot be a differentiator among your equally capable colleagues to be on your manager's boss' radar. Your skills, strengths and achievements must be visible by your manager's boss and that is your responsibility as well as your manager's.

If you have already had some discussions about your career with your manager, and don't see outcome, you can request your manager to let you meet his boss. If your manager suggests that you be patient for some more time then do listen to him. However, ask him for some timeframe for waiting. If still nothing happens, you can broach the topic again and set up a meeting with your manager's boss if the issue is still open. Always make sure that you keep your manager in the loop. Never do it behind his back because that could backfire on you.

Employees usually set up such meetings after they have missed an opportunity. The secret is to find out about such opportunities beforehand. So the best thing to do is to make sure that your manager and his boss both know about your aspirations. Again, this is why it is important to develop a relationship with your manager's boss, not just when you need something, but even when you don't need anything. Your career can also get a boost when your manager's boss chooses you to lead a cross-functional effort reporting (not a change in reporting structure, but interacting closely for the project) directly to him for the duration of the project. Even if this is for a limited period, do not hesitate to take it up. When you think about growing vertically, don't just look for certainty, a permanent role or change in designation. This will make you miss out on short-term opportunities and might hinder your growth. If you execute such projects well, you have a higher chance than your peers to get a permanent role in the future.

A word of caution: your manager's boss may give you a couple of opportunities, but if you are choosy and turn them down without proper reasons, these opportunities will stop coming to you, and after a few attempts you might be considered as a closed person. Therefore, it is important that you should first know what you really want and show flexibility in taking up something that may not help in your short-term career but will pay rich dividends in the long term. Many a time, to grow you need to make a lateral movement and take up challenges that are directly not in your domain or line of business.

> *Your manager's manager needs to know who you are and that is best accomplished by stretching yourself beyond your normal duties in ways that are more broadly impactful, in other words deliver quality work and then deliver more!*
>
> ~MICHAEL FRENDO, EXECUTIVE VICE PRESIDENT, WORLDWIDE ENGINEERING, POLYCOM INC.

35. APPRAISING THE APPRAISAL

When a manager submits salary and compensation data for his team, his boss will look for an overall sanity of the data. He can go through the full list, generate reports to look for anomalies, if any, and also to ascertain a fair distribution of the budget. However, it is also true that he will pick a few people and review their cases thoroughly to ensure that the manager has appraised them correctly. These few people are normally those who matter the most due to their performance; criticality of the project; or those who have raised issues in the past; or even those who are prone to attrition due to the market condition or those who were lower in the salary bracket for some reason, etc. It is important that your name is foremost on his mind so that you are picked for a review. Most of the time your manager's boss will agree with what your manager has suggested, but during compensation rationalization, your manager's boss needs to ensure that certain employees are taken care of well.

He will question your manager, if his suggestions do not match with his impression about you. For example, if your performance rating was less than what he thinks you should get, it is his prerogative to ask your manager to provide the data or give examples to support the case. One disadvantage of your manager's boss knowing you too well is that if the rating given by your manager is higher than what he had anticipated, he can question your manager to find out the reason for the high rating. There is a probability of him reducing the rating, unless convinced by the reason provided by your manager.

He will try to facilitate the normalization process across teams to ensure consistency—ensuring that no manager is being too strict or too generous. When the time for salary hike comes, he provides a second pair of eyes for a select few to ensure fairness. This is really helpful because the HR normally provides a salary range and a guideline on the hike in a generic way and will only raise questions when there is some gross violation of a guideline. The manager's boss provides fairness in a more specific way as he will have better pulse of the team than the HR. However, when the budget is tight and the industry is in doldrums, the manager's boss would ensure that the selective few are well taken care of, even if he has to impinge on other employees' share. Are you one among the select few?

Your manager may recommend performance bonuses or awards for employees but accepting the recommendation is his boss's prerogative. So having a good understanding with him goes a long way in helping your case.

What Can You Do?

If you have doubts or concerns about your salary, appraisal or performance rating, you first need to take it up with your manager. If you are not satisfied with his responses, you could explore two options: either accept it with a pinch of salt or approach his boss. Your manager could himself suggest that you to talk to his boss. If you haven't built a relationship with your manager's boss, and are meeting him for the first time, you need to think through what you want to say. Position the conversation by briefly introducing yourself and your contributions: be humble and explain how it is unfortunate that your first meeting with him is for reconsideration in your appraisal or salary hike.

Normally these decisions are not solely decided by your manager—he acts only with the consent of his boss. So don't go with any expectation of corrections because a majority of the time, it does not happen because these things are well thought through. Your best chance is to get a fair assessment before the process got kicked in. Ensure that your manager and his boss are aware of your contributions. Don't assume that they will know everything about you. Go ahead and meet with your manager's boss to put forward your case. If things have already been decided, they would keep in mind your points for the next cycle. Try and avoid taking the conversation to a level you will repent. Also, be ready to receive feedback whether you agree with it or not.

It is possible that your manager has pushed your case and his boss might not have agreed. In such a case, which you may be unaware of, it is a good idea to provide a summary of your achievements and your expectations clearly, so that if your manager's boss has played a spoiler's role, he will be more careful in the future and may try to undo some of the damage. In the rarest of rare occasions, the manager's boss could ask for more details and work with the HR to rectify the error.

A word of caution: everyone makes mistakes—it could be your manager or your manager's boss. Ensure that you don't stretch the discussion beyond a point. Instead, focus on your assignment with enthusiasm and passion. If you find the same things happening repeatedly, then the message is clear that there is a mismatch between what you think about yourself and what the management thinks about you. Either you can decrease your expectations and work on improving yourself based on the feedback they have given you or you could change your team or company. It would be better to improve on your performance or behavioural issues or whatever is suggested in the existing team because there is no guarantee that you won't land up in a similar situation in a new team or company.

> *Organizations generally like to normalize the decisions across a broader spectrum of people at the same level. This often means that the manager's manager is involved in decision making. It is prudent to make sure that your skip level manager is aware of your activities and achievements so that he/she has correct data points to make a relative judgment.*
>
> ~AMIT PHADNIS, PRESIDENT ENGINEERING AND INDIA SITE LEADER, CISCO SYSTEMS

36. HELP!

Like most people you too can go through ups and downs in your life. There can be some phases in your life during which your career may take a backseat. These could be due to personal circumstances like taking care of your children or ailing parents. It could be health issues or difficult situations like a complicated divorce or a personal financial problem. These difficulties can distract you, which could cause disruptions in your career. Your attention will get divided and affect your deliverables, which in turn will impact your performance ratings. When you are going through such a phase in your life, it is normal to expect some kind of support from your organization.

Managers normally reach out to HR to find out if there is precedence in accommodating such requests, but most of the times, the situations are so unique that they require a separate consideration. In such circumstances, the manager's boss has wider discretionary power than the manager and he will use it to extend help. However, as these are not well-defined, and managers are sympathetic to every employee, still a person's contribution, his standing in the team and criticality in the organization help in getting a better consideration in this hour of need.

Even if you may not want to divulge the full details of a problem to your manager and manager's boss, you need to take them into confidence to sensitize them about the gravity of your situation, if you expect some understanding and a solution from them. As these things are not covered explicitly under any HR policy, the management has to justify to the HR any such recommendations and work closely with them for a tailor-made solution. These solutions will tend to differ from person to person due to their unique circumstances therefore due diligence is always done by the manager, his boss and the HR together.

What Can You Do?

Keep a list of options handy to discuss with your manager. Your options could range from a reduction of work hours till you feel confident about getting over your personal crisis. to a reduction in your responsibilities or a transfer to a role that is less demanding. You could also request for leave without pay for a certain period or some other time bound options. If you are not sure about anything, leave it open ended with the onus on you to inform your manager when your crisis is over. You can revisit it after a few months as mutually agreed. Whatever you choose, you need to be cognizant of the fact that your original role or responsibility might be given to someone else. When the crisis is over you need to be patient to get back similar or better opportunities.

All managers would like to extend help to a needy employee. However, they also need to convince the management and the HR before doing so. You can offer to present your case to his boss and HR. Your manager will appreciate it irrespective of whether he needs your help. He wants to somehow find a win-win situation and to save a potential attrition.

A word of caution: you might be in a situation of distress and are thinking about taking a break from the job to take care of your other priorities. You are aware of the financial challenges you will face in not having a job, but you go ahead and announce your resignation without exploring any other options. Quitting may be the only option, but before taking any hasty decisions, discuss with your manager to find a win-win solution. Difficult situations are not always personal: they could be work-related too. These include new customers, price negotiations, new product launches, high quality time bound deliverables, customer complaints, tough quarterly or annual goals. Here too, the manager's boss could provide valuable inputs and suggest ways to achieve it. He could even go beyond and provide you with the right contacts to benefit both you and the organization. Sometimes your manager's boss can understand your challenges and will not come down that heavily on you if you miss your numbers. He may even set more realistic goals the next time round!

> *During one of my career stints, I was managing a BU that was selling and implementing ERP solutions. We were trying to win our first Baan account in India and were pitching our solution to a customer in South India. We entered this account quite late in their decision*

> cycle and the prospective customer was already in the final decision phase. We needed an opportunity to present our proposal to the top management of the company. My boss suggested reaching out to his boss who could reach out to the customer and request for a meeting to be set up. This meeting was set up and we were able to demonstrate the efficacy of our solution and ultimately won the customer order.
>
> ~USHASRI TIRUMALA, SENIOR VICE PRESIDENT AND GENERAL MANAGER, MANHATTAN ASSOCIATES (INDIA) DEV CENTRE PVT. LTD

37. A VIEW FROM THE TOP

Companies do encourage skip level meetings wherein your manager's boss can call for a one-on-one meeting with you. He can also call team members for a meeting without their managers. Such meetings are done in the absence of managers to enable employees to speak up freely.

Such meetings are important and should be encouraged so that your manager's boss can spell out his vision and hear the team members directly. If any project is running into trouble, your manager's boss may want to hear about the issues directly as well as the suggested solutions to be able to assess the situation correctly. Sometimes these meetings are called to motivate team members to help them through the difficult phase of the complex nature of their work.

These meetings are also helpful for your manager's boss to get a pulse of the team or of a person, and can help him to sense anything that could be brewing in your team or a person. He can quickly alert your manager to stop a potential problem from turning into reality. He could also read the issue with a different perspective and help your manager in dealing with it. Such meetings and interactions give team members a chance to resolve issues and help in clearing doubts and sometimes, to learn about future plans too.

The manager's boss calls these meetings not for manager bashing but to tap the right pulse and appear more accessible to team members. If in such meetings, your manager's boss senses that an issue is directly related to your manager's decision, management style or behaviour, then he needs to take it up with the manager.

It could be an indirect way of taking a 360-degree feedback on your manager. It could also be to verify any doubtful data your manager may have given.

These types of meetings are planned, but what about the unplanned ones?

What if your manager's boss just drops by your seat and asks you a specific question or calls you to his office alone or with others at a very short notice and without any specific agenda? What if he asks you something in the hallway? All such meetings or encounters could make you nervous if the asked questions are controversial.

On one hand you might feel that you have arrived and that you are one of the chosen few who have been contacted for some valuable input, but on the other hand there is fear of being misquoted because you don't have a clue on the ulterior motive behind the questions.

What Can You Do?

Whenever such meetings are called you start worrying about: what to say and what not to say; whether your manager will come to know about it and how he will react to it. Whether anything you say will be used against him, will that make you his sworn enemy?

If it is a small team meeting you tend to feel a little less worried because others can do the talking and this can save you from any controversial statements. But the flipside is that you will miss the opportunity of getting the right visibility! You should speak in such meetings not as a union leader but to put forward the facts as you see them. In one-on-one meetings too, you give cursory responses that may not help your manager's boss in picking up issues and he might conclude the meeting earlier. Again you missed the opportunity to impress your manager's boss!

First of all, you should not be worried about such meetings. If you are self-confident and have the right grip on the area of your work, and also have a bigger picture, you are ready. You can answer confidently about what you know. Hopefully your answer is not a surprise to your manager because there is always a possibility that your manager's boss will cross-check with your manager. If you think you have spoken something which might surprise your manager, then do update him.

You can also ask question to your manager's boss. No question is silly; no issue is small, if it is bothering you, you must ask. If nothing is bothering you, you could even ask a question to get information, but make sure your question should not be of mundane routine stuff but of his level for example, future plan, risks which he foresees, his assessment of certain issues, etc. You could ask for any clarifications you need or give suggestions and definitely volunteer for additional work if you have bandwidth. Other questions you can ask are about upcoming projects; about his impression on your team; and also about his suggestions on how you can grow. He may not be prepared to answer all your questions and may sidestep a few, but at least he might think about them. Make sure that it doesn't turn out to be a cribbing session—mix it with what is going well and what else can be done. Stay positive.

The dilemma is when it is well known that your manager and his boss belong to different camps ideologically. If you are ideologically aligned to one stand then make it clear. Avoiding this situation might show that you don't have a stand and therefore you are not worthy of taking any senior position. If you don't have a clear stand at least provide pros and cons of the two stands and try to explore a middle path, which will tell them that you are mature in your thinking.

If you are forced to speak about anything sensitive, be honest and speak in the right tone giving examples to support your statements. Sometimes some questions are politically loaded and you may be put in a spot where you have to say something. Again, speak your mind or ask for some time to get back after thinking through what you will say. Once communicated, if you feel your manager should not know about something you said, make it clear to your manager's boss. This will put a bit of psychological pressure on your manager's boss about quoting you. If you have said something that you want to change, send him a well thought-out email. A smart thing to do would be to update your manager on what you have spoken about.

But what happens if your manager's boss has a hidden agenda against your manager? What if he is trying to use you to pin down your manager for something? You might feel a shiver down your spine because you know what's cooking, but you have to show maturity in speaking the truth, without any exaggeration or sugarcoating and stick to what you say. If you don't have the full picture, then provide information on what you know without extrapolating or deducing conclusions unnecessarily. If you chicken out from such a situation, you will appear timid or immature. As you grow in your career, you will land up in even more complex situations where you need to deal with issues that are not just black and white, but grey too.

> *Modern organizations build and sustain a culture of open communications and it is important to ensure that communications can break hierarchies when required without any undercurrent of politics.*
>
> ~GANESH NATARAJAN, VICE CHAIRMAN AND MD,
> ZENSAR TECHNOLOGIES LTD

38. MANAGER AND YOU

Every relationship goes through its ups and downs. Sometimes these lows are short-lived and sometimes they could stay longer. If you feel that in spite of all your efforts, your manager is not doing enough to end your woes, your normal response will be to find a new manager. Even if it finally turns out to be the only option, you need to explore other means of making your working life better which includes approaching the manager's boss.

You may feel hesitant to go to your manager's boss with your issues because you may feel that your manager and his boss are hand in glove about everything. Even if it could be true, there is no harm in finding out.

You need to realize that there is a pressure on your manager to improve his relationship with you too. The burden on your manager will be higher if your performance and contributions are widely respected. The pain for your manager becomes even more acute if you are well networked. Your manager might fear his own unpopularity as people's sympathies are mostly more with the employees rather than with them! Even if you enjoy excellent rapport with your manager, there will be times when the manager might not be doing or acting in your best interest. It is worse if you don't know when your manager is going against you, so you are neither prepared nor equipped to handle it. Some examples of this could be when your manager does not give you the credit that you deserve and instead hold you responsible for some mistakes in communication to your manager. He may not recommend you for some important role as he fears losing you from his team. He could also feel threatened by you.

Sometimes it so happens that once you start building a good understanding with your manager's boss, your manager starts acting in a weird way with you because he is feeling threatened. He might try to badmouth you or downplay your achievements. A good interaction with your manager and his boss, and fine balancing to overcome such situations is an art and must be developed for any career growth.

A mature manager will always welcome a good relationship between his team members and his boss because by doing so he is seen to be transparent in his actions. He will be at peace because his boss will not be surprised about any people issues or work challenges due to his good networking with his team.

What Can You Do?

You have only a few tools in your toolbox to face the first situation: First and foremost, continue doing the great job that you are doing, as most of the time when your mind is clouded with such feelings, it is easier to get distracted and frustrated and this can impact the work and make your situation even worse.

Next, you need to approach your manager for a direct discussion on the issues that you are facing and to clear misunderstandings that may have cropped up between the two of you. Listen to his feedback and suggestions and try to work on them.

If the situation does not improve or the response is not satisfactory, set up a meeting with your manager's boss, preferably after informing your manager. Here are two scenarios:

1. Your manager's boss does not have any inkling of any disagreement between the two of you. In this case he will listen and may want to buy time to discuss the issue with your boss. Try not to just give only your side of the story, but provide as many perspectives as possible because that will speak well about you. Once you summarize the problem, provide a few solutions too and seek his support in choosing the right one. Then, request for the

next meeting to discuss what happened so that you are not kept in a limbo.

2. If your manager has already updated his boss, listen to what he has to say. If he just parrots what your manager has already said, then you will understand that there is no point expounding your case further. If you remain patient and positive, once he is done with his explanation he might ask for your suggestions. You could give him options to reflect on and choose from, and leave it at that. Give him some time to think about it. Again, set up a follow-up meeting to close the issue. Always be prepared for a status quo, but don't give up trying. If not this time, he may be more receptive and supportive the next time around.

Your requests will be given a more serious thought if you are a great performer and trustworthy. You may think that there is no point going to your manager's boss because he shields your manager. He may shield your manager in your presence, but in his one-on-one with the manager, the story could be different. He would have more data points about your manager, his dealings with the other team members, and his dealings with his peers, and most importantly your manager's dealings with his own supervisor. If he sees merit in your case and it is in line with his own observations, he will question your manager and ensure that something is done. If it is something totally new, he will ask your manager to find out something or provide a viable timeline for the closure of such an issue. He would also try to come up with a response to you in agreement with the manager. Even if the response might be not in line with your expectation, keep in mind that you have informed the right person and that when the time or opportunity comes, he will keep it in mind and act in your benefit. The onus also lies on you to be patient and not keep checking on the progress frequently. If you are known to be a high-maintenance person or a habitual dissatisfied person, then chances of something coming out positive for you could be bleak unless your request is trivial and can be fulfilled easily.

In the second situation, where you don't know what is happening behind your back, you cannot do anything. The only thing is to have a good relationship with your manager's boss who knows your contributions.

A word of caution: when you don't know your manager's boss all that well when you take up matter with the big boss it could prove to be counter-productive. Keeping your poise will certainly help as an outburst or irrational statements will bolster your manager's stand. You will have lost the battle before it is even fought even though you may have valid concerns. Don't exaggerate your own issue. Don't take the names of the people who might be facing similar issues, as they might chicken out when asked, thus making your stand weak. Stick to the issue that you are facing.

As your manager's boss knows your manager quite well, he will look at an issue from various perspectives by keeping your manager's weaknesses and strengths in mind. He can work as an enabler to mend the relationship between you and your manager.

If the relationship between you and your manager is strained for a long time with no sign of recovery in spite of taking it up multiple times with the manager's boss, then quitting could be an option.

> *Assumptions, pre-conceived notions and communication gaps are often the root causes of concerns related to alignment in the workplace. Think of your working relationships inside an organization. Ideally you want to cultivate a professional network across all levels—and this should include people in your management chain as well. If you feel strongly about something, talk to the right people about it. Remember, the only bad question, is the one that is never asked.*
>
> ~UJJWAL SINHA, VICE PRESIDENT, ENTERPRISE BUSINESS INTELLIGENCE AND ANALYTICS, TARGET CORPORATION

CHAPTER SIX

MANAGING MANAGER'S PEERS

39. SEEKING SPONSORS

Networking with your manager's peer is very important in your work life. It is also one of the most powerful catalysts in your career progression. How can it be a catalyst? When you are on the right side of the manager, your manager will push your case and will get support from his peer. If you are on his wrong side, this relationship can help kindle a hope that all is not lost. If this is so simple then why don't people try and bond with their manager's peers? The answer is simple: inorance and lack of tact.

Most people are ignorant as they think it is a different team, and the manager of that team will not have any say in someone else's career and compensation. The area of work under that manager is of no interest to the person. There is hardly any need for any interaction to complete the assignment.

Those who understand the importance of such relationships

may have started to build them, but they fail due to their tactlessness. This tactlessness could be something like divulging the team's internal sensitive information to the manager's peer, thus landing the manager in a difficult situation. It could also be that the person offers some help voluntarily to the other team by not keeping his manager in the loop. Your manager would not like to be at the receiving end and could come down heavily on such employees. Rather than learning from the mistake and becoming more tactful, the employee's first reaction is to start distancing himself from the manager's peer to avoid antagonizing his manager further. Therefore only a smart few who nurture such relationships with tact can reap dividends from them in their career.

If your manager's peer has better rapport with his boss than your manager, then it is even more important that you nurture the relationship.

What Can You Do?

Your work might not require any interaction with other teams, or you may not be interested to develop any relationship without purpose because you are a junior, but remember that it is important to build and nurture such relationships. Some smart people keep looking for such opportunities and when they see a challenge in their team that necessitates interaction with their manager's peer, they volunteer to go and speak.

Another important thing to prioritize in your career development is skill improvement. This relationship will also help in broadening your knowledge as you will learn about things happening in the other teams as well. This will not only enhance your visibility, but also open doors for any future opportunities in that team or elsewhere.

As you grow in the organization, you become aware that during staff meetings of your manager's boss where all those who directly report to him are present, many points are covered, including discussions on new opportunities, appraisals, promotions, issues, and many more. A good relationship with your manager's peer can help you to advance your prospects because he will recommend your name in such meetings. Crises, failures and challenges are also discussed at these meetings and if you are on good terms with your manager and his peers, you could be shielded from undue blame. If you are at fault, at least there will be someone who can also speak up for you by giving your side of the story.

Seeking your manager's peer as a mentor or adviser is a very good career move. A good manager will not mind you networking with anyone in the company because he knows that it could be useful for him too. For example, if any issue crops up with another team, you could be asked to help in solving it due to your good relationship with them. This could also help you get a sense of not only new projects, but also those that might be having issues. In turn, you could put proper checks and balances in your own work or in your team so that a project that spans multiple teams goes smoothly.

A word of caution: any relationship can have its own ups and downs and so can the relationship between your manager and his peer. This is where you need to be tactful. The thumb rule is to make sure that you don't weaken your manager's position through your statements and actions.

> *There are inter-dependencies in your managers' peer group. Networking with them can help release some bandwidth off your manager, and that's what you need to genuinely accomplish. That way your manager doesn't feel uncomfortable or threatened and in fact welcomes your initiative. This gives you an opportunity to engage and influence people who are pertinent to your career. Remember: promotion and bonus pools are limited and one needs sponsors other than your reporting manager to be successful.*
>
> ~ANUP RAU, CHIEF EXECUTIVE OFFICER, RELIANCE
> LIFE INSURANCE

40. BUILDING BRIDGES

Managers need help too! If your manager is trying to push your case for better responsibility, a new role, a promotion or an award, he may have faced some resistance from his peers. This is where support from your manager's peer(s) will certainly help. Sometimes both your manager and his peer have an understanding about supporting each other's candidates—this is where your relationship with your manager's peer matters because he will choose you over others.

Then there are times when your manager is not in his boss's best books. In such cases, your manager's peer's support for you is extremely important. If your manager has tried various ways of doing something good for you, and it is getting stuck at higher level, his peer may be able to help him. In such cases, even you could reach out to your manager's boss or manager's peer too for a positive result.

There could also be times when your manager is uncomfortable with his peers and may not want to interact with them on controversial topics. In such situations, he might ask you to take it up if you have a good relationship with them. The manager will be happy that he does not have to put pressure on his already strained relationship with his peer(s). Some managers could turn such situation into their favour by claiming to groom you to take more challenges and to interact with people at higher levels; and in turn, he could be looking for more challenges from his boss.

What Can You Do?

Helping your manager goes a long way in improving your relationship and it is one of the key ingredients for your success.

You can become a saviour for your manager by getting him the required support from his peers. If you have a good relationship with your manager's peers, you could be much sought after to defuse the crises that involve your manager's peer(s) teams. Your role in such situations becomes more visible if your manager and his peer are somewhat operating at a dysfunctional level which is evident to others.

You can also help in your manager's ambition. If he wants to take up additional responsibilities but fears the lack of support from his peers, you can volunteer to help your manager. Let him have the ownership of the project, but let him get it done through you because you have a good relationship with the other teams. Of course, whatever rewards he gets will benefit you too. Some 'hierarchical' managers could portray to their boss that it is his team member who is dealing directly with his peers, meaning that he himself is a notch above his peers.

> *A great tip which is normally not known to many, as many fear having a good relationship with manager's peer will antagonize the manager, but on the contrary the manager's peer can help the manager in pushing the employee's cause.*
>
> ~RAMKI SANKARANARAYANAN, FOUNDER AND CEO, PRIME FOCUS TECHNOLOGIES

41. SAFEGUARDING YOUR INTERESTS

When your manager's boss calls for a meeting to discuss the performance rating of his team, each of his direct subordinates including your manager will present the data for their respective teams. Once presented, it is open for discussion among your manager, his peers and his boss. Sometimes managers present borderline promotion cases, and if his peers support it, those people can move up. If you fall in such a category, you will need support from your manager's peer(s). Although every manager would like to have his team get the lion's share of rewards/promotions, the whole purpose of the meeting is to ensure that there is consensus and the manager's boss is the driver in such discussions.

The question that might come to your mind: when people are force-fitted into different performance categories as per the HR guidelines, why should your manager's peer recommend someone from another team rather than someone from his own team? Although there is no fixed number assigned to each team for every performance category, each team will have some people who could fall in a higher performance bracket. A manager's peer can suggest that a person be reconsidered if he is not in that manager's list. This might irk your manager, but if his peer presents examples to make his point strong, he'll just have to go with the flow. Such discussions will also help the peer to project himself better to his boss showing his keen networking skills. If your manager is not well prepared with his own data, he will be forced to do his homework better and will take such cases more seriously in the future.

Sometimes the peer might compare his own person against someone in another team. Generally all managers try to portray their team members as better than the others, but it is not always true. If the peer portrays you as a better performer than his own borderline performer, then your manager will be forced to take a second look. Your manager's position becomes more vulnerable if other peers also join the chorus in supporting you.

Under difficult situations companies do need to reduce their headcount. This is usually performance based or otherwise. These are the most difficult times for any manager. Again here too, every manager prepares his own list and then it is discussed at the staff meeting with the manager's boss. The list is scrubbed multiple times and many rounds of negotiations take place to minimize the impact. During all such discussions, strong support from your manager's peer could help to save you or borderline employees from being laid off.

A manager's peer can help employees in other ways too. As his interactions are wider and he is privy to more information, he could catch insights or detect warning signals about an employee and can provide suggestions to you on what to look out for, when to keep a low profile or which relationships to improve. Such advice can be really useful, and can help you to rectify yourself before any issue snowballs. But shouldn't it be your manager who should be giving such feedback? Yes, but he may not give you direct feedback to avoid hurting you. He will dilute the message and this does not have the required impact on you. It may also be the case that you are so used to receiving feedback that you tend to treat it as just another one and do not attach enough seriousness to it. Your manager purposely may not provide you feedback because of your past indifference with it.

If you have no direct communication with your manager's boss, and feel that your manager might not be communicating your case in the right light, you could approach your manager's peer to get your point across.

What Can You Do?

Normally one's manager is fully aware of the informal networks of each and every member in his team. If you are linked and associated with people whom your manager considers 'heavyweight', then he will think twice before taking any adverse steps against you. So the first step will be to reach out to your manager's peer and develop a good working relationship with him.

The next step is to make sure that you apprise your manager's peer of your achievements and challenges objectively. This will help him to defend and support you when need be. You can go even further and ask him to be your mentor. If he accepts it, you can update your manager too, to make your relationship with his peer more formal and transparent.

A word of caution: your manager's peer might probe you to get information on your team. If it is harmless, then there's no problem, but if you feel such information might put your manager in a weak spot, think twice before sharing as you lose your manager's trust. You need to maintain a fine balance. There is no point in making a new relationship at the cost of the present one.

You can handle such situations by replying to your manager's peer in many ways: 'It is better you ask my manager', 'My perspective might be different from others', 'I have limited knowledge of the issue', etc.

However, if you feel strongly about something and are in command, you can share it with him and stand by your statement.

> *Multiple strong relationships strengthen your career, and association with your manager's peers can help enhance your visibility, immunity from politics and growth path.*
>
> ~RAKESH SINGH, VP AND GM, CITRIX INDIA

42. REACHING OUT

Everyone looks at challenges from their own perspective and that is true with your manager too. He may not very open about updating his team members on what is discussed at management meetings. He just informs the team about what needs to be done. No project, assignment or challenge can be looked at in isolation, and this funnelled information flow hinders the full picture required to execute it. Normally an all-hands meeting by your manager's boss or someone even higher in the management ladder can help you in understanding the importance, but even such meetings are infrequent and therefore, frequently changing dynamics can be captured only when you are equipped with more information.

This is where the manger's peer is useful. A probing question from him in the hallway could alert you to the importance of something that you probably might have not attached much significance to. Another way to find out the importance of something is by taking the opinion of your manager's peer.

When you hear anything about your team or company through the grapevine, your manager will most probably not respond to such comments, as he will want to wait for communication from the management. This is when the manager's peer can be of help depending upon the nature of the news. He could advise you to watch out for something or may just ignore it. His body language and the official response will help in making your own judgment based on this additional information.

What Can You Do?

You should try to get as many perspectives as possible, as it helps in understanding the problem completely. Most of the time people are just bothered about their own part of the work, and therefore they lose the bigger picture. Various perspectives can not only broaden your understanding to solve the challenge in a complete way, but also help you in sensing potential opportunities. You can take it up with your manager when you see an opportunity, thereby taking a lead against your peers This type of far-sightedness is required at all levels and your manager's peer is one of the best sources to get you information.

Sometimes your manager may trap you by praising the usefulness of the current assignment when he knows that you are dying of boredom. By getting another perspective you will come to know where your project stands against other projects.

In some teams or divisions, there is a bad culture of hiding information. As the organization becomes more dynamic and changes take place faster, it is important to equip yourself with many perspectives to avoid being caught off guard at events that can impact your career directly or indirectly.

> *Most of the real world important problems are multi-dimensional in nature. The solution that you are providing will be more appropriate if we understand more dimensions of the problem space. An important dimension that I have seen adding value is the perspective from the peer of one's boss. It reiterates the management viewpoint and sometimes gives additional perspectives that are important but not fully understood well from the boss. Personally I have seen several good leaders effectively using this avenue.*
>
> ~SANTHOSH KUMAR, PRESIDENT AND MANAGING DIRECTOR, TEXAS INSTRUMENTS INDIA

43. IDENTIFYING YOUR FALLBACK

In the fast changing work environment, you can never be sure that you will not need a fallback. If for any reason, you are finding it difficult to stay in your present team, your relationship with your manager's peer is your key to escape! If you have the required skills, you can approach him to help you migrate to his team.

The reason for wanting to try out a new team could be many, such as you are bored with your current team as you have been part of it for long; or wanting to try out something new in the same company. It could also be an opportunity to rise faster. Another reason for wanting the change could be an interesting project that has come to the other team and the manager of that team is ramping up his team. Of course, a big reason could be that your relationship with your own manager in the existing team is not at the level you want to and you feel more comfortable with his peer.

Although at most times, your manager will support your move, but there is a greater chance that your manager may be upset about you wanting to leave the team and could escalate it to his boss. It is therefore up to the manager's peer to impress upon your manager and present your case to allow the transfer. Your manager could also feel that you are closer to his peer and therefore leaving the team is a good move for you.

What Can You Do?

In order to get the maximum returns on having a great relationship with your manager's peer, it is important that you improve your networking skills. You will want to communicate things about yourself to impress him. There's nothing wrong in doing this—telling him about yourself, your aspirations and your challenges and seeking his opinion. But you are missing out one important aspect. What is happening in his team? What is the plan for his team? Can any of your ambitions be satisfied by joining it? Such questions will motivate you to identify additional skills that you may need to acquire for your growth. Once you start understanding their work and processes and are equipped with their work knowledge and challenges, you can have discussions with his team members at equal footing and can give solutions to the team of your manager's peer or directly to manager's peer. This too will increase your respect. The manager's peer will see more value in you and will also start seeing benefits in nurturing such a relationship because the key to any good relationship is that it should be mutually beneficial.

> *Developing a good relationship with the manager's peer is very important, both in good and bad times. Most of the time, the realization comes when the situation is already bad, and by then it is too late to build such relationships.*
>
> ~RAVI GURURAJ, PRESIDENT,
> NASSCOM PRODUCT COUNCIL

44. ROADBLOCK

Your manager's peer may not always a helpful person, but can also put obstacles in your way. These obstacles could vary from situation to situation. For instance, if your manager is recommending you to take up a visible role where you have to closely interact with the team of the manager's peer, your manager's peer can resist the change, and instead suggest another person he knows well. If your manager insists, you could still be taken in, provided he's heard positive things about you. If you have already interacted with his team and the impression is not positive or you have a reputation of not being an 'easy' team player, then the manager's peer might put his foot down and not accept it.

If your manager is recommending anything related to your career progression that could trigger a comparison or competition within other teams, your manager's peer will be more careful. If they don't know anything about you, they might want to buy time to observe you before your manager can recommend you again. Don't look at it like an obstacle, but as a temporary setback. You could argue that your manager has neither built your case properly nor coached you well in advance, but look at what you have not done for yourself first.

A neutral image of you in your manager's peer's eyes might help. However, lack of any type of image will not help if you are aspiring for a leadership role. Here, only a positive impression will help.

What Can You Do?

It is important that you realize the importance of your manager's peer and try to build a positive image of yourself. Use any opportunity to let him know about your strengths and seek his help in overcoming your weaknesses. Most of the time, you might not be working directly with your manager's peer. In such cases, building a right perception about yourself is critical. The peer can form an opinion about you by observing you in meetings, seeing your presentations, observing your relationship with colleagues and other such activities. He could also ask his team members how you interact with them or he could hear it from your manager. But this doesn't mean that you need to be good with everyone all the time. It just means that you should be known for what you stand for. Your soft skills play a major role here. Once in a while everyone has their bad moment, and the management understands and realizes it, but if you have an annoying nature, for example, a habit of passing the buck, or always accusing others for mistakes, being discourteous, or not being a good team player, then it is better that you improve upon such areas before you look for a cross-functional role or growth opportunities.

Sometimes, it might not be clear even to your manager on why his peer(s) are not supportive of a wider role for you which involves their team too. In such cases, you can offer to talk directly with your manager's peer to find out the issue and work towards it. Usually, managers provide feedback on your improvement areas and relationships you need to focus on.

> *When you encounter somebody who doesn't want to bet on you because they don't know you or like you, don't be pushy. Instead, get inside their heads, learn what matters to them and reframe your goal in way that relates to their problems. This approach works every time!*
>
> ~SHARAD SHARMA, CO-FOUNDER, ISPIRT

CHAPTER SEVEN

MANAGING OTHERS

45. BE ON THE RIGHT SIDE OF THE HR

You like most people subscribe to the notion that the HR department of your organization cannot help you. You may have a long list of woes: Your salary hike is not up to your expectations. It unnecessarily force fits during appraisal. HR policies are inflexible. Even if your manager wants to do something better for you, it raises concerns. The HR keeps rolling out policies in quick succession and sometimes it causes confusion as these overrule the previous ones, which everyone was just getting used to. The list does not end here.

It is important to understand the reality behind such woes. Most of the time issues come in various hues. What managers want are specific examples to handle a given situation. As no two situations are the same, there is no one-size-fits-all remedy, and this is what causes the confusion. In these conditions, the manager and the HR need to work closely to ensure consistency in following the practices as much as possible.

As the HR is part of a company's support organization, therefore even if they are doing something good in the background for any employee, the credit may go to the manager who is front-ending the team. However, when something doesn't go well, the blame always falls on the HR, even some managers tend to portray it like that.

The HR can moderate all difficult people-related issues raised and is in a position to suggest solutions. Such solutions can range from mild to severe actions and can vary depending on the situation. Your manager can help in finding a solution which is less impactful for you. The only instances when he cannot do anything is in extreme cases like sexual harassment or discrimination, where if the guilt is proved, termination is the only option. Laws against sexual harassment are stringent and it is important to understand them clearly. Inappropriate insinuations, jokes, photos or videos can land you in trouble. Remember that this is not just restricted to the office, but also in office-sponsored events like offsites, parties and other activities. Today all companies have set up committees to look into such issues and decide accordingly.

Your manager is the person who decides your promotion and compensation, but the HR too plays a major role. Sure-shot promotions are sometimes denied by the HR or objected to if they have definite proof of unacceptable behaviour. In cases like these, they ask the manager to evaluate their decision by monitoring the employee, and give a promotion only when it sees an improvement. The manager could also be questioned by HR if they find any anomaly in the promotion or compensation.

When an employee is going through a rough patch in his personal life and needs the company to support him, the manager seeks help from the HR in determining the level and type of support. The HR also works on relocations, transfers and other aspects that are not only essential, but also beneficial for employees.

What Can You Do?

If you are facing an issue where you need help from your manager and the HR, fix a time to meet them. Don't try and hide or twist the information to make it favourable for you because that could create more problems. If you have made a mistake, admit it. Listen to what they say. Maintain your version correctly and don't keep changing it depending on who you are talking to. If you keep in mind these points, then there is a fair chance that your issue will be considered.

Some people either become abrasive or their tone becomes accusatory. They will blame everything and everyone else but themselves. They don't realize that sorting out a problem amicably is the only way out. The manager can use some of his discretionary powers to minimize the impact of the situation, but only once they are convinced about the employee's needs.

When sometimes neither the manager nor the HR wants to go an extra mile—it is mainly due to three reasons:

It is beyond their scope to entertain such requests. It could also be that the employee's image is not good or his behaviour in the past has not been up to the mark, his story is not reliable, or anything else that the HR and the manager consider reason enough not to go an extra mile for. The third category is when both the HR and the manager feel that entertaining such requests might open a can of worms, and therefore they do not want to do it without any change in policy.

As your dealing with the support team is occasional and mostly through your manager, it is even more important that you deal with it in an appropriate way. Wrong perceptions can be carried on for a long time given the infrequent nature of interaction. Such perceptions can get passed from the support team to your manager. Your manager may choose to ignore it but if reoccurrence is a possibility, then he may provide a feedback to you. In serious matters, your manager will be bound to act upon the HR's recommendation. In such cases even your high performance and good relationship with the management will take a back seat.

The HR can either be your saviour or it can cause you the most pain. It all depends on how you build your relationship with the HR, directly or indirectly.

> *HR is the best neutral party and your partner to solve your career equations.*
>
> ~BHUVAN NAIK, VICE PRESIDENT HUMAN RESOURCES
> INDIA, SAP INDIA

46. BIG BROTHER IS WATCHING YOU

Most organizations these days provide laptops to employees to be used at the workplace and at home. Some employers also give company phones for ease of business. Typically, all company-provided devices have software that captures all the activities that you perform on such devices. These are important to protect intellectual property and the confidentiality of the company. The software logs not only all activities but also active file transfers through emails or USB ports, uploads or downloads, web-surfing activities and a lot more to catch anything being done surreptitiously.

Many companies also have their own IT guidelines that incorporate country-specific IT policy requirements and global requirements if the organization is a multinational, and all the employees need to adhere to them. Major violations are dealt with very seriously and sometimes termination is a possibility, and minor violations lead to warnings.

Most companies have equipped themselves with tracking and monitoring software too. As soon as you enter office and swipe your card, the data is captured. Cameras installed at common areas take pictures and store them too. But this does not mean that there is a person sitting and sifting through such records every single day. Companies keep these records based on their own policies, which are also influenced by the country specific guidelines. So if and when there is an issue, such recordings can be extracted and looked at to ascertain the facts. Requests for doing so can come from HR, IT, management or from the facility itself. Sometimes these recordings and data are required by the government for a lawsuit or as part of a probe and the company is bound to provide the data.

Employees need to be cognizant of this fact and adhere to company rules.

What Can You Do?

Employees who abide by the employee handbook or company policies have no need to worry. If for certain reasons you need to take some deviations, you must first seek your manager's approval. For example, there are some who consistently cannot meet their required number of working hours at work, which without explanation or prior approval can become an issue. If you want to access a website blocked by the company, but you need it to complete a task, then seek your manager's approval rather than figuring out ways to bypass the rules. If the company is generous and does not put restrictions on the use of internet, the onus comes on you to adhere to its policies.

You need to take prior approval for installing any unauthorized software on company-owned devices. You may want to try out many new things on your computing devices to experiment. It is fine if it doesn't harm the installed software. Those who are in the software industry need to be careful in using even public domain software, as prior legal approval needs to be taken for this too.

You should also be aware that any personal emails if sent and received via the official mailbox is also open to scrutiny. Sharing inappropriate jokes or pictures with your colleagues or friends by using company property is against your company policy and can land you in trouble.

Another important point that could impact you is posting inappropriate comments on social media sites using your company name or email address. Never do so unless you have been designated as the company's spokesperson. There is no harm in putting your personal views on topics related to work as long as you use your personal email id and conceal your office name. When in doubt, always check with your manager or concerned person in the company.

Doing the right things when someone is watching is compliance—doing the right things when no one is watching is responsibility. Right use of digital privileges is our responsibility.

~RAMASWAMY NARAYANAN, DIRECTOR GLOBAL IT
AND CENTRE LEADER FOR MEDTRONIC, BENGALURU

47. A PENNY SAVED IS A PENNY EARNED

The finance department plays an important role in controlling a company's expenditure. Any suspicious expense(s) without prior justification are subject to scrutiny. Typically, the finance department sends such filing(s) to managers to seek their opinions. So if you have taken a unilateral step in incurring expenses that are outside the company policies after having taken prior approval from your manager, but he had failed to inform the finance department about it on time then your manager is liable to give a justification on why he approved such an expense.

This can frustrate you because you had taken prior approval. Please understand that there are checks and balances put into the system to avoid financial irregularities and this is the reason for such scrutiny.

Your company may have a policy on gifts too. It is a major issue if you are in a role in which receiving and giving gifts is common. Any irregularity on this front can have a major impact on your career, even leading to termination if the finance department or management gets a whiff of dealings which are over and above the policy guidelines.

What Can You Do?

There are three types of situations which you can face. You could be stuck in an unknown place during an official trip and you are not sure about what you can do. You may use the company credit card for personal expenses, and you may not be in a position to wait. Sometimes you may end up spending office money out of sheer ignorance. Before you go ahead with the expense, reach out to your manager, the HR or the finance department through a phone call, SMS or email mentioning what you plan to do before you actually act. Even if you don't get an immediate response, you have done your duty to inform them of the circumstances and your decision. This is acceptable.

The second scenario is temptation. You may feel that the company will not be able to catch certain expenses, so you spend the money. You may even go further and forge expense reports or commit frauds and plead ignorance if caught. Be ready to face dire consequences when you are caught. It is not whether the amount is big or small but the intention that matters.

The third situation is when you have a feeling of 'entitlement'. You may think that as you have worked for long hours or on weekends, or have unwillingly travelled on company work and so you can claim 'ignorance/absentmindedness' on account of being preoccupied with work and therefore, forgot to follow certain procedures. You justify this because you are wired into the 'entitlement' mindset. In such cases the management might be supportive and possibly sympathetic of the situation. However, if they find out beyond doubt that you are using work pressure as a tactic, they will come down on you heavily. Your reputation may be damaged for good. So just because you escaped once, does not mean that you can repeat and get away with it again.

> *We the finance professionals as the conscious keepers of our organization, need to ensure that each penny spent is a penny earned for the organization, all within the duly approved process. Any expense, even if permitted by the organization policy, should be incurred only if it is rational and essential. Any minor fraud, could have major consequences for the organization, if it goes undetected. Also, financial impropriety of whatever quantum can have a long-term adverse impact on one's career. Globally, financial impropriety is a punishable offence.*
>
> ~SANJAY BERRY, SR VP FINANCE AND CORPORATE
> CONTROLLER, BHARTI AIRTEL LIMITED

48. CUSTOMER IS THE EMPEROR

Every company considers its customer as the 'emperor', so mishandling the 'emperor' has dire consequences. Hardly any employee will knowingly make mistakes on this front but it is only a few who have the art to manage their customers well. It is not sufficient to just have non-complaining customers or their representatives, it is necessary that customers' expectations are met properly and that they are engaged not only throughout the period of the contract, but before and after too. All kinds of issues can flare up—deliverables that do not meet expectations, miscommunication or misinterpretation of messages or ill-timed or negative messages. Not only do these require major damage control, but they affect the trust built over so much time. If more effort and time are spent on controlling the damage, this might not bode well for you. Your career can take a hit if a customer or his representative complains against you or if you become a scapegoat in the internal politics of the company and are forced to withdraw some of the verbal commitments you made to a customer or if you have overstepped your brief and gone ahead to win over the customer at any cost without any backing from your company. Beware of these pitfalls as you will be left alone to fight your battle.

A few smart people can play the customer card to their advantage. They are good at customer management and their management depends on them not just for the negotiations at the beginning of the project, but also throughout the engagement period. They are also roped in for damage control if any, due to their special skills. For them, if the customer is in their pocket, they can negotiate any amount of benefits from their managers at the appropriate time. They are aware of their unique skills and the impact of them leaving the project, team or even the company. Sometimes such movements of employees from their existing roles are questioned by the customer. On one hand, a manager will try to have alternative channels with the customers to reduce dependability on a few people; while on the other hand, such key employees who enjoy a special relationship with the customer get the maximum benefit from his management.

What Can You Do?

It is important that you are very careful with your customers. Make sure that your communication is precise and accurate without any ambiguities. Sometimes people go overboard and spill more than the required information—things that the management is unwilling to share with the customer. It could also be overcommitting to something the company has not authorized you to do. Your enthusiasm to share more sometimes gives a premature peek into the company's roadmap, which is not for public consumption and may not be taken well by your company. Some go even further and wash the dirty linen of internal politics in front of their customers. If you have unknowingly done any such thing, be sure that your maturity will be questioned. You might be first counselled, but if there is a repetition, then slowly you will find yourself being replaced in spite of your great relationship with the customer.

Sometimes you fall into situations in which you are forced to make a commitment to your customer without getting the chance to check with your manager. Your company might not support your commitment making you vulnerable in front of the customer. This will not go well with your management either. Whenever a shrewd customer traps you to agree to something, it is important that you buy time. Keep your management updated on the precise nature of your communication to avoid coming in the crossfire later.

When management reviews your case from the role, responsibility, compensation or promotion perspective, they keep your special skills in mind. However, when the manager feels that his arm is being twisted, it can leave a bad taste.

If you are friendly with your customers you might try to get recommendations or verbal appreciation from them just before appraisal to strengthen your case. Although managers appreciate such emails, they also know the purpose very well. So it is important that you don't go overboard collecting recommendations. If a manager senses that you are too smart a player, he will start looking for an alternative channel with the customer to reduce dependency on you.

Even though all customers are important, there could be some who had bigger accounts which have shrunk for any reason, and they no longer are part of the key accounts. If you are handling such an account, your fortune might take a fall too. Try and keep a balanced approach in customer management both during good or bad times. Keep you management in the loop so that they understand that there could be things beyond your control.

While it is important to build a good relationship with the customer, be prudent. You walk a thin line between the customer and the management so don't take this skill for granted, as with every interaction your skills are tested again and again.

> *Keeping customers happy is a cornerstone of a successful business. Always be the customer's champion within your organization and continuously strive to delight your customers with everything you do.*
>
> ~HARI VASUDEV, SVP ENGINEERING, FLIPKART

49. KNOWING YOUR VENDORS

If you are responsible for vendor management then vendor management is another important skill that you should hone. Negotiation, communication and execution are the key skills for such a role because the person in charge of signing or finalizing the contract gets fully involved in upfront discussions and negotiations before handing it over to the team that has raised the request. The same person might also be the one who will manage the vendor during the execution of the project, and he could be you. Never make the mistake of assuming that vendors will get the deliverables as per your expectations on the required date. Knowing that the project is in jeopardy, you may blame the vendor for not meeting the deadlines. At this point, the management will certainly try to help in minimizing the impact of the delay by setting up escalation meetings with the vendor to iron out the differences. But they will also put you on the block. If you have not made things clear or not provided the right support, the vendor can also become offensive and escalate the matter by showing all the proofs.

Signing the contract with a vendor is not an abdication of your responsibility, but the beginning of your responsibility of ensuring that you get the high quality deliverables in a timely fashion. This is the key to successful partnerships. There could be a change in the circumstances from the initial understanding due to some reasons, such as the vendor having his own set of problems, new data warranting some changes, changes in priority from your side, and so on. If you do not escalate the issue on time to your own management and to the management in the vendor organization, you will probably be held responsible for mismanaging the project. This will definitely not go well in your short-term career, and you will need to wait for another chance, if any, to prove yourself.

What Can You Do?

The minute you sense an issue with the vendor during any intermediate milestones or otherwise, you must ask the right questions to get to the bottom of the issue and also keep your management aware of what is happening. Never hesitate to ask probing questions, thinking you are the master, so vendors need to come to you with their challenges and update you. If you are not getting satisfactory replies, or are suspicious about the responses, ask for a face-to-face meeting or escalate it to the vendor's chain of management to get a reply.

Communication plays a very important role here. There are many surprises, such as a change in requirement, misinterpretation of order, unclear dependencies, and so on. A mechanism to exchange information and manage such changes or surprises is the key to keeping both parties in sync. Failing to communicate key changes such as changes in priority can have a huge impact on the deliverables.

Vendors are integral part of an execution strategy. Never fail to realize this. Never treat vendors in an offhanded way, thereby not giving them the full picture and the importance/criticality of the project. That not only leads to mismatched priorities, but also causes aloofness in team members where they don't feel being a part of the larger project ecosystem. Hence, the vendor's part in the chain should be tracked just like any other in-house items.

Vendors are partners. For a partnership to be effective it's important for the people to like each other, at a high level have some sort of congruence in which they see the world and have a shared value system. Outcomes don't have to be 'managed' and life becomes easy when we choose who we work with carefully. And once we find them if we focus on making the journey together and enjoying it together, we may find that the journey is really the point.

~DEV AMRITESH, PRESIDENT AND COO,
DUNKIN' DONUTS INDIA (A DIVISION OF
JUBILANT FOODWORKS LTD)

CHAPTER EIGHT

MANAGING THE ACROBATICS OF FUTURE

By now it must be clear to you on how to manage the various stakeholders in your workplace, each of whom plays a direct or indirect role in your career growth. If you are able to manage such relationships well you will be able to fast track your career in comparison with those who have similar or better domain knowledge, but lacked such skills. You work in a complex matrix environment where your project's success is dependent on many others who may not be in your immediate team. If you can handle the challenges of such management with ease you can win the race because matrix management is basically dealing with various relationships in order to get the work done.

There are some positions in the company which require persons good at managing relationships. Also there are various situations in the company where such people are high in demand. For example, a customer complaint which requires finding the root cause of an issue across groups and also to pacify angry customers. However, managing such relationships can become more effective when people realize how to manage and improve themselves.

The tips discussed in this book will help you grow in your career, but that will be incomplete if you are not cognizant of a few realities plaguing this century.

Reality 1: As per the Eurobarometer Survey Report of 2011, 'Since 1960, life expectancy has climbed by eight years and demographic projections foresee a further five-year increase over the next four or five decades. Needless to say, our retirement age has also increased over the decades.'

Reality 2: The long-term relationship between organizations and its employees that existed in the past has taken a huge hit. Neither employees have the same level of loyalty towards their company compared to the previous generation, nor do companies have the stability to provide long-term job guaranty.

Reality 3: In the recent past, many reputed and branded behemoths fell within few quarters or years. Many correlate growth in career with making more money. Therefore, under such an unpredictable environment, employees want to earn more in less time and are always on the lookout for ways to increase their earnings. This new trend is to provide a cushion due to the job uncertainties in the increased longevity era. However, many don't succeed because on the one hand, one's working life has got extended, and on the other, organizations are becoming slimmer and flatter by cutting through hierarchical levels and consolidating job functions. This means fewer jobs and therefore, fewer opportunities to grow and a smaller chance to earn more in a shorter span of time.

All this might lead to a complex career crisis in the future. For example:

Hari started his career in his early twenties, and being a high performer, he climbed very quickly and became Senior Director in his forties. His colleagues and friends consider him a high flier and he was proud and happy with his achievements. He continued to work hard but after a few years, sensed that even after giving his best, there was no higher he could go in the foreseeable future. With around twenty more years to be in active employment, he doesn't want to believe that the Peter Principle will be applicable to him so soon. The Peter Principle states, 'In a hierarchy every employee tends to rise to his level of incompetence.' This means that employees are promoted to senior levels due to their competence, but at one stage they become stagnant because they cannot be promoted further as they are no longer competent for a senior position.

Hari feels that he has all the skills his boss has, and knows that he has a fair chance when his boss quits, but he also knows that he cannot plan his career based on his boss's exit. Frustration sets in as he faces stagnation. He, of course, fails to realize that his boss might be in a similar situation too—neither is he bad at his job to be fired nor can he retire soon. Even though Hari firmly believes that his career is in his own hands, he is clueless. Unknowingly he too is blocking the growth of people below him. So in spite of how good he is, and even if he jettisons his ambition, it is impossible to hold on to the current job for the rest of his work-life due to the uncertain nature of organizations these days where mergers, acquisitions, closures and lay-offs have become the norm. He knows that a junior equipped with better skills than him might soon replace him.

Hari sometimes thinks about becoming an entrepreneur but he neither has any concrete ideas nor do his current financial responsibilities allow him to do so. He has huge impending expenses like the expensive college education of his kids and the need to save for his retirement. He leaves things in status quo while keeping an eye on the job market and waiting for a dramatic turnaround or a stroke of luck to get the job that will advance his career.

What is Hari's underlying fear?

How can he be meaningfully employed in his current job for a long period even if he cannot rise?

How can he be equipped to deal with life when he is without a job, but still has years left in his work-life?

50. YOU ARE A PRODUCT

It is important for you to realize that you are a product and that you should plan your career in the same way companies strategize about product life cycles. So it is worthwhile to study a typical product life cycle in any organization and try to apply some of the learning points to your career. Graph 1 is a typical product life cycle chart.

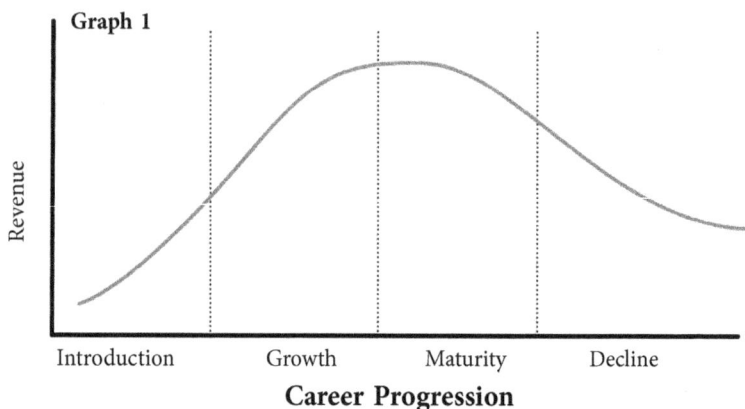

Career Progression

Introduction Growth Maturity Decline

Source: Author.

The first phase is the introduction of the product into the market. After some time, it picks up and sees a growth phase. Over time, the product reaches its maturity where returns are maximized. Finally it enters the decline phase.

Your career follows the same pattern. The growth curve rises to a peak in your career. The peak is reached while a significant period of active work life still remains, so it is natural for you to be concerned about extending the maturity phase to as many years as possible to be able to earn more.

What Can You Do?

What do organizations do in order to get the maximum return from a product? They want to keep it at the maturity phase as long as possible. How do they do that? The normal strategy is to add more features to the product—called 'mid-life kickers' so that it still remains an attractive product in the market. For example, any well-known product comes with various version numbers where each version has an additional feature. The features could be physical like the look, feel, colour, or size, or better capabilities like faster operations, longer life, ease of use, etc. Similarly, if you think of yourself as a product, adding more skills—more 'mid-life kickers' can extend the maturity phase of your career and allow you to remain valuable to your employer for an extended period.

How can you add mid-life kickers? Learning is a lifelong process and in this modern age, you need to acquire new skills faster, due to the advent of technology and fast changing circumstances. Depending on your industry, you need to look around and gauge what skills people who are in the early stage of career are getting equipped with. Evaluate whether you can manage or lead your team with the skills that you have or do you need to learn new ones to ensure that you are respected and able to do your job well. This is the most important tool that will help to extend your working life. Graph 2 depicts how adding new skills can extend the maturity phase (the dotted line) and thus extend employability.

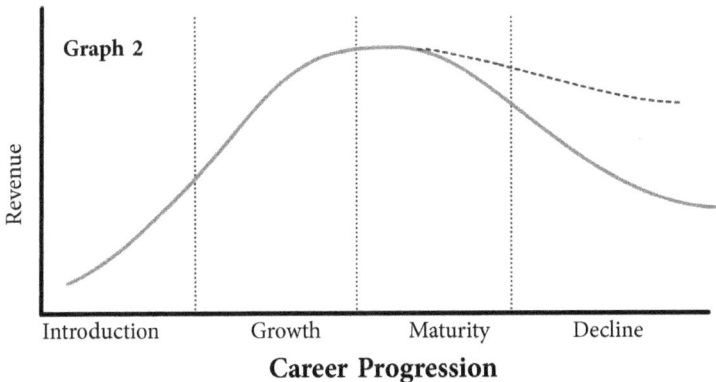

Career Progression

Source: Author.

Many people realize the need to extend their maturity phase by learning new skills when they are already in decline and that is too late. This happens because in the late maturity phase people fall into a 'cash cow' situation where they become complacent in their roles, as without learning any new significant skills they could meet or exceed their manager's expectations. They don't see the need to change because things are going great for them as it is. The manager is also happy to have low-maintenance people who can be 'milked' for as long as possible. People fail to see that the world is changing fast and that they might soon become obsolete thereby triggering a decline phase earlier than expected. This normally comes as a shock to many. They tend to blame the organization, while forgetting that it would like to have multiple 'cash cows'. Although organizations invest in skill improvement in their workforce, the onus lies on the employee to extend its maturity phase.

> *Don't underestimate the necessary learnings through each stage of your career. From the fundamentals that build the foundation in the early years through reinvent-ment in the later years–each stage will present its own set of impediments and achievements which will uniquely prepare you for what's to come.*
>
> ~STACEY SALAZAR, VICE PRESIDENT HUMAN
> RESOURCES, INFINERA

51. EXTENDING YOUR SHELF LIFE

As life expectancy increases, the retirement age is getting pushed back further and further. On the contrary, people are trying to achieve things faster at a younger age with minimum patience. This poses another challenge for you: how to keep working till the retirement age. To extend the maturity phase mentioned earlier, you can extend it by add new skills though there is no guarantee that you will not enter the decline phase much before retirement. Remember that the work tempo has increased and you will reach your career peak (or the maturity stage) earlier.

What Can You Do?

Again, let us go back to what an organization does when it foresees a decline in its product. Much before the decline of an existing product, a company launches a new product. The revenues from the new product together with the revenues from the existing product increase the company's top line. See Graph 3.

Graph 3

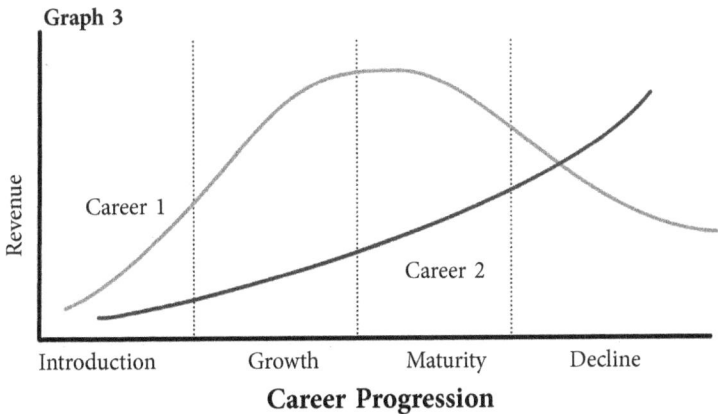

Career 1

Career 2

Revenue

Introduction   Growth   Maturity   Decline

Career Progression

Source: Author.

A company's transformation from a one-product company to a firm with a large product portfolio can reap rich dividends. Apply this to your career to stay relevant. How can you become a product portfolio?

The answer is simple though complex to accomplish. As work lives have been extended, it has become easier to have multiple careers. This is possible provided you understand the two pillars necessary to support this objective: first, the courage to start from scratch; and second, the ability to harness a hidden passion that can be monetized.

These multiple careers could be inter-related. Say for example, a senior executive can be a management trainer too, or a cricket player can become a cricket coach. These careers could also be completely disconnected. For example a person in the IT industry could start an advertising agency, or a person in a consulting firm could start an NGO.

There is no right or wrong time to start a second career. Most people realize the need for it when they are either already in the decline phase or out of a job. This leads to disruption and sometimes forces them to take up something just to pay the bills or to buy time to decide what they can do next, even if that role is a step back in their career plan.

As you can see from Graph 3, any new career needs to start much before the decline phase is reached. This is important because this gives you the chance to experiment with new ideas before taking the plunge. Furthermore, it gives you enough time to develop and refine the strategy and gain the required skills and advice from before taking the final plunge.

This begs the question, when it the right time to switch careers? There is no good or bad time. It all depends on your preparedness, your current career stage, and your familial and financial situations.

Another question arises is whether your company will allow you to develop the second career. This depends on its policy. If it is a simple decision like an executive writing a book, it might be allowed, but if it is about him starting a management consultancy then it may be disallowed. It is always safe to seek permission from your employer before you start a new venture, even if it is something like putting up a painting exhibition where you can make some money.

While introducing multiple products, an organization's effort is always aimed at increasing the top line, but when you are switching from one career to another, there is a possibility that you might need to take a hit from the compensation perspective. This could be temporary or permanent. However, you need to be happy that at least your second career has provided you with a new lease of life with passion and optimism.

> *Like products which have survived generations, you need to reinvent yourself every 5–10 years.*
>
> ~KRISHNAKUMAR NATARAJAN, CEO AND MD,
> MINDTREE LTD

ACKNOWLEDGEMENTS

I would like to thank N.R. Narayana Murthy for endorsing the book. I am also thankful to the fifty-one industry leaders who have shared their insights. Their views are given in their personal capacity and are not a reflection of their companys' stand.

I would also like to thank Divyank Rastogi, Shekhar Bhide and Krish Verma for providing valuable comments and suggestions in this book, and Dibakar Ghosh of Rupa Publications for challenging me to think beyond the finish line. I am grateful to my parents, my children and my wife for giving me the time and space to write this book. Most importantly, I would like to thank the readers of all my earlier books. It is your encouragement, comments, appreciation and inputs that have encouraged me to write this.

www.ingramcontent.com/pod-product-compliance
Lightning Source LLC
Chambersburg PA
CBHW031933190326
41519CB00007B/511